HEALTHCARE MERGERS, ACQUISITIONS, AND PARTNERSHIPS

AN INSIDER'S GUIDE TO COMMUNICATION

David Jarrard

In partnership with Geisinger Health System

HealthLeaders Media
A Division of HCPro

HCPro

Healthcare Mergers, Acquisitions, and Partnerships: An Insider's Guide to Communication is published by HealthLeaders Media.

 5 4 3 2 1

ISBN: 978-1-61569-249-1

HCPro, Inc., provides information resources for the healthcare industry.

HCPro, Inc., is not affiliated in any way with The Joint Commission, which owns the JCAHO and Joint Commission trademarks.

David Jarrard, Author
Karen Kondilis, Editor
Jim DeWolf, Editorial Director
Matt Cann, Group Publisher
Doug Ponte, Cover Designer
Mike Mirabello, Graphic Artist
Matt Sharpe, Production Manager
Shane Katz, Art Director
Jean St. Pierre, Vice President of Operations and Customer Relations

Advice given is general. Readers should consult professional counsel for specific legal, ethical, or clinical questions.

Arrangements can be made for quantity discounts. For more information, contact:

HCPro, Inc.
75 Sylvan Street, Suite A-101
Danvers, MA 01923
Telephone: 800-650-6787 or 781-639-1872
Fax: 800-639-8511
Email: *customerservice@hcpro.com*

Visit HealthLeaders Media online at: *www.healthleadersmedia.com*

06/2013
22038

Contents

About the Authors

David Jarrard

David Jarrard is a recognized expert in healthcare transaction communications and CEO of Jarrard Phillips Cate & Hancock, Inc., a healthcare public affairs firm that helps hospital leaders use communications and political thinking during times of significant change. With offices in Nashville and Chicago, the firm is among the largest healthcare public affairs firms in the United States.

Over the past 20 years, the professionals at Jarrard Inc. have built and managed more hospital partnership campaigns than any other healthcare public affairs firm in the country. Learn more about the firm at *www.jarrardinc.com*.

Contributors

Susan M. Alcorn has spent her career leading marketing and communications for hospitals and major U.S. healthcare systems. A public relations and marketing consultant based in Washington, D.C., she recently served 14 years as chief communications officer for Geisinger Health System, a $4 billion integrated health services organization in Pennsylvania. She is also a past chairman of the American Hospital Association's Society for Healthcare Strategy and Market Development (SHSMD).

Kevin Phillips is a founding partner of Jarrard Phillips Cate & Hancock, Inc., and has led communications for more than 50 hospital M&A campaigns over the past 15 years. A politico at heart, he spent more than a decade working in national politics both as an administration staffer and on local, state, and presidential campaigns.

Molly Cate is a founding partner of Jarrard Phillips Cate & Hancock, Inc., and brings more than a decade of experience in media crisis communications and corporate campaigns. She author's the firm's widely-read newsletter, *Inside Baseball*, which covers the storied Nashville healthcare community. Previously, Cate covered Nashville's $70 billion healthcare industry as a business reporter.

Anne Hancock Toomey is a founding partner of Jarrard Phillips Cate & Hancock, Inc., carrying significant experience in hospital M&A, reputation, and certificate-of-need campaigns. She previously served as head of communications for a surgical facilities company, managing day-to-day as well as high-stakes initiatives for the organization.

David Jolley, APR, is vice president for system public affairs at Geisinger Health System. He has been instrumental in the organization's messaging and strategic public outreach throughout the past several decades, particularly as the organization has added five hospitals in the past nine years to its integrated care network.

Kristen Hayner is a senior executive advisor with Jarrard Phillips Cate & Hancock, Inc., focusing on the interplay of politics and messaging in grassroots, organizational change, and M&A campaigns. Previously, she worked in speechwriting for national political leaders and as a press secretary in the Tennessee General Assembly.

Acknowledgments

The guide you hold in your hands reflects wisdom gleaned from working closely with board members, executives, and communication leaders at hospitals big and small across the United States over the past 20 years. We are deeply grateful for the opportunity to have worked with them during some of the most important moments in the lives of their hospitals.

The best practices (and frank warnings) found inside were written by a few, but are drawn from the experiences and sharp thinking of the many talented professionals within Jarrard Phillips Cate & Hancock, Inc., and Geisinger Health System. Thank you to all!

Special appreciation goes to contributor, book director, and field marshal Kristen Hayner. Without Kristen's organizational savvy, leadership, and tenaciousness, this guide would simply not exist.

In addition, we greatly acknowledge the vision of Dr. Glenn Steele, who has led Geisinger Health System for more than 12 years. Through his leadership, Geisinger has become a national model for how healthcare is delivered and financed, and has helped define what successful partnerships can be.

Last, thank you, dear reader. We sincerely hope you find this book an invaluable guide for helping you lead your organization through these extraordinary times.

Introduction

If your hospital is pursuing a strategic partnership, we've been where you are.

This guide represents the distilled wisdom of a team of experienced healthcare communications professionals who have helped healthcare organizations across the nation tackle the toughest partnership communications over the last two decades.

Many healthcare professionals contributed their experience, insights, and technical expertise to this guide. Among these professionals is more than a century of healthcare communication experience. Mergers, acquisitions, joint ventures, alliances, sales ... we've seen them all.

Turning that experience into strategies and tips for the nation's hospital and health system communicators is what this guide is all about.

In this time of unprecedented change—marked by more partnerships than ever before—we believe this guide is a much-needed resource as our industry navigates through this era.

Section 1

COMMUNICATING THE BIG DEAL

The Communicator's Guide

You hold in your hands a communicator's guide written specifically for hospital leaders whose organization is partnering with another healthcare system, whether buying, selling, or something in between.

> Not a hospital leader? Are you rather leading a health system, group practice, sub-acute care organization, or other healthcare organization? Keep reading—this guide can help you, too. You will specifically be interested in "Partnerships Old and New" later in this section, which highlights how smart communications can aid even the most simple of new arrangements between providers of patient care.

This guide is designed to offer tried-and-true, practical advice for one of the most difficult communications challenges you will ever face.

Communicators often do not get an early seat at the table when transaction work gets under way. This guide will help you jump-start and sustain your efforts as your hospital or healthcare organization faces one of its most critical moments.

The Urgent Language of Today

Merger. Acquisition. Partnership. Joint venture. Affiliation. Collaboration. Alliance. Holding company.

This is the urgent language of healthcare leaders today.

Old rivals are joining forces; community hospitals are welcoming out-of-town partners; not-for-profits are converting to investor-owned facilities; major regional systems are aligning; national systems are acquiring. Some are looking to expand, others to join something larger. Organizations that wouldn't have even dated a few years ago are now getting married.

Experts tell us that big scale and broad scope are essential for success in the swiftly evolving and dramatically changing healthcare marketplace.

However, it's not just about size. It's about caring for your entire population through a system that is more integrated, more complex, more cost-sensitive, and more demanding than ever before. Thoughtful hospital executives and trustees are taking action today to ensure their health systems survive and thrive in this new world.

The result? We're experiencing hospital realignment on an unprecedented scale. Every organization today is a potential partner, buyer, or seller. Consider these statistics:

- According to a 2012 *HealthLeaders Media Intelligence Report*, nearly 80% of healthcare leaders said they would have merger and acquisition deals under way or would be exploring deals over the following 12–18 months.
- Recent figures from Kaufman, Hall & Associates, Inc., an independent management consulting firm based in Skokie, Ill., that provides advisory services and software to hospitals, health systems, and other healthcare entities, show there were 106 hospital transactions announced in 2012, compared to 83 in 2010 and 101 in 2011.

Everybody's playing. This is not merely the story of independent, stand-alone hospitals being targeted as likely partners for bigger systems. Major and regional systems are in the hunt today for true partnerships that will strengthen them for tomorrow's demands. New super-systems and national brands are being born.

In short, if a health system isn't doing it, they're thinking about it. This includes your hospital or provider organization.

A Glimpse of the Future

Partnerships are the future of healthcare delivery.

This includes partnerships between hospitals, between regional health systems, between hospitals and physicians, between providers and insurers, between hospitals and pre- and postacute care facilities. Each brings unique strengths and specialties that span the continuum of care.

When these entities work in true partnership, the result can be a seamless healthcare experience with better quality offered at a better price and through a better experience for patients, staff, and physicians. This requires making structural changes, such as common IT platforms, shared finances, and a host of operational synergies.

But, in a sense, that's the easy part. These partnerships also require a fundamental cultural shift among physicians, nurses, professional and support staff, and the communities they serve.

It'll be a bumpy ride, but we will get there as an industry—the marketplace, the government, and empowered consumers will drive us there.

As professionals who have dedicated our careers to advancing the delivery of quality healthcare, this shift of tectonic plates affects every one of us, each of our professional colleagues, and the patients whose lives we are called to serve.

This guide will help you contribute to the future we must build together.

A Road Map for Communications

Hospital partnership communications are a tremendous challenge. The task requires a different way of working and thinking. If you have never been down this road before, it can be like driving at night without headlights.

Think of this guide as a map that can take you safely through your initial communications strategy to the closing press conference and all the way through the post-close campaign. It includes tips, recommended tools, and warning signs, all offered to help you stay on track along the way. For additional updated resources, visit *www.partnershipcommunications.com*.

How to Use This Guide

This guide includes several key sections that—when put together—can help your partnership's communication strategy and build your plan.

Each section blends high-level strategy with practiced, in-the-trenches advice and to-dos that will help any hospital communicator and leadership team communicate well.

This first section includes an overview of key components of the book and how they fit together to create your plan. A critical piece of this is acknowledging that, while partnerships are taking on new and innovative forms, the communication principles remain the same. So whether you find yourself in a traditional merger of two in-market competitors or creating a relationship between a provider and insurance organization, this guide is a resource to you.

> See "Partnerships Old and New" later in this section for more on this idea. It's really about thinking of our industry in terms of a new sense of "we" (who we are together as an industry) acquiring to expand out, not just bring facilities and services into an insular fold.

Next, we dive deep into the terminology and step-by-step overview of traditional deal terms and how a traditional hospital merger works. Every partnership is unique, of course, and the rules will vary depending on state laws and regulatory oversight. But, in general, this overview will give you a sense of structure and a timeline around which you can begin to build your plan.

> We include an expanded glossary of critical deal terms at the end of this book.

Then we discuss how to think about partnership communications. Partnership communications require a holistic communications effort. Everything and everyone matters because everyone and everything in your hospital is affected by this defining event. We offer a model for approaching your plan.

Finally, we turn to the heart of this guide: the rules. These are 10 road-tested rules for making partnership communications successful. Each rule offers:

- **The Big Idea:** a discussion of the rule, why it matters, and what can happen when the rule is violated
- **Take Action:** a practical next step and the key component to help you get there

Next, we round out the book with attention to some specific issues you're likely to face in your partnership communications planning. This starts with a discussion about digital media, helps you troubleshoot specific scenarios, and then discusses what to do after the papers are signed. Last, we address steps to take in the event your partnership fails to go through even after the announcement.

In each case, it's important to remember that every health system partnership faces its own unique situations. In Section 3, "Troubleshooting: What to Do When …," you will find specific pointers for managing some common yet incredibly challenging scenarios. These include:

- Faith-based to secular conversion
- Not-for-profit to investor-owned conversion
- Name change
- Antitrust concerns
- Public referendum
- Facility repurposing

Although you can use the rules as a foundation to your communications plans, you may need to finely tailor your work to your organization's specific needs.

At the end of the book, you'll find case studies of real partnerships that took place throughout the country over the past 10 years. In each case, leaders dealt with multiple issues throughout the life of the partnership, and used communications to help their organization succeed.

Put together, the information in this guide will provide you with a platform for building your initial communications plan and practical advice to help you move through the process.

> Every day, our landscape is changing. You'll find the authors' latest observations on these transformational changes, thoughts on navigating them, new rules, and other commentary on our website, *www.partnership-communications.com.*

What's the Big Deal?

To build an effective communications campaign, you need to know how a hospital partnership deal comes together and how to think about the transaction as a whole rather than simply a series of disconnected, event-driven milestones.

Now, stop.

Before you jump to the partnership rules, spend a few minutes reading these pages and getting familiar with the terms and timelines of a deal, as well as a sense of how partnerships can be structured. Doing so will help you ask the right questions to build your plan.

Today's Healthcare Partnerships

The architecture of hospital partnerships has become increasingly creative as organizations work to customize their partnerships to meet their needs. Depending on the debt structure, legal and regulatory restraints, community needs, relationships with physicians, cultural needs—any number of factors—partnerships are as unique as the hospitals and healthcare organizations they bring together.

How does a healthcare system partnership transaction deal come together? It depends on a few things, such as:

- The structure of the partnership. There are many: Mergers, acquisitions, and joint ventures (JV) are among the most common, with creative variations of each popping up here and there.

- The state laws and regulatory approval each state uses to provide oversight of a change in hospital ownership or control.

Caveats aside, there are common definitions and steps to just about every hospital partnership transaction that you need to know to build an effective communications plan.

Large-scale, successful multihospital mergers are becoming more common. According to Kaufman Hall, the median net annual revenue base of the merger partner has increased from approximately $97.7 million in 2010 to $137.0 million in 2012, representing a growth rate of approximately 38%. The number of merger partners with annual operating revenue in excess of $1 billion has increased from three in 2010 to eight in 2012. Four of the eight 2012 transactions involved a $2 billion participant, compared to just one in the previous year and three over the past two years combined.

Top 10 Partnership Terms to Know

The following are not legal definitions, but are, instead, practical uses of each term. You'll find more terms in the glossary. Kaufman Hall provided a review and framework for the graphic representations of these terms.

acquisition: This is the outright purchase of one hospital by another healthcare system or company. Control clearly shifts to the acquiring hospital, which will often have committed to invest money, infrastructure, or expertise. The introduction of a new culture, new systems, and new standards are to be expected in an acquisition. Figure 1 shows a commonly used framework for an acquisition.

FIGURE 1

FRAMEWORK FOR AN ACQUISITION

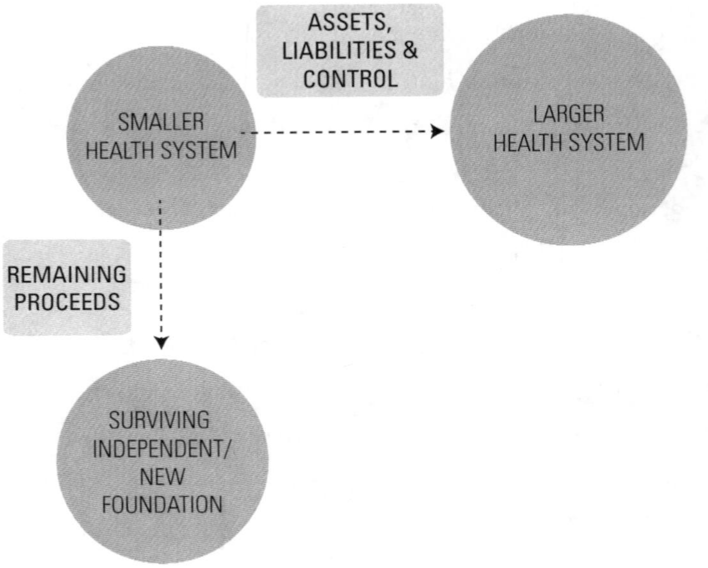

affiliation: More focused on collaboration, this is a partnership arrangement that stops short of any acquisition or purchase. The goal is mutual benefit rather than creating or changing identity. Often, the partnership is centered on making improvements to each hospital that the hospitals could not, or chose not to, develop on their own. Figure 2 shows a commonly used framework for an affiliation.

FIGURE 2

FRAMEWORK FOR AN AFFILIATION

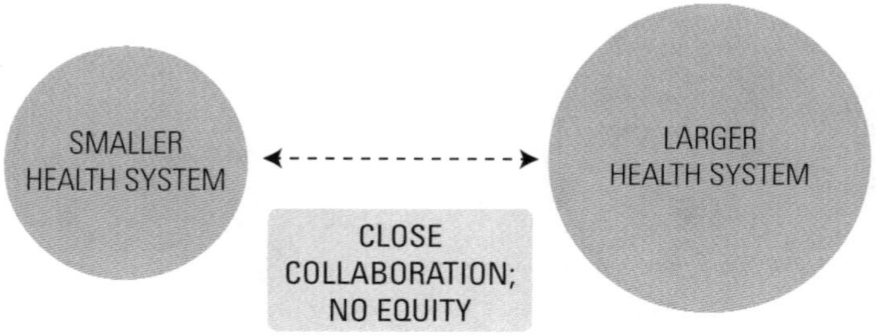

merger: A merger occurs when two organizations agree to contribute most, if not all, of their assets and liabilities—buildings, cash, and receivables as well as debt and outstanding claims—into a new, combined organization. Equity is sometimes equally shared—a 50/50 deal—or the ownership in the new combined system reflects the value each organization brings to the table. Who will govern and control a newly merged entity is always a key question to resolve. Successful mergers require a true spirit of cooperation. Sometimes acquisitions are called mergers in press releases, but don't confuse the two. If control shifts heavily to one partner, it's a merger in name only. Sometimes there are political reasons to say "merger" rather than "acquisition." Figure 3 shows a commonly used framework for a merger.

FIGURE 3

FRAMEWORK FOR A MERGER

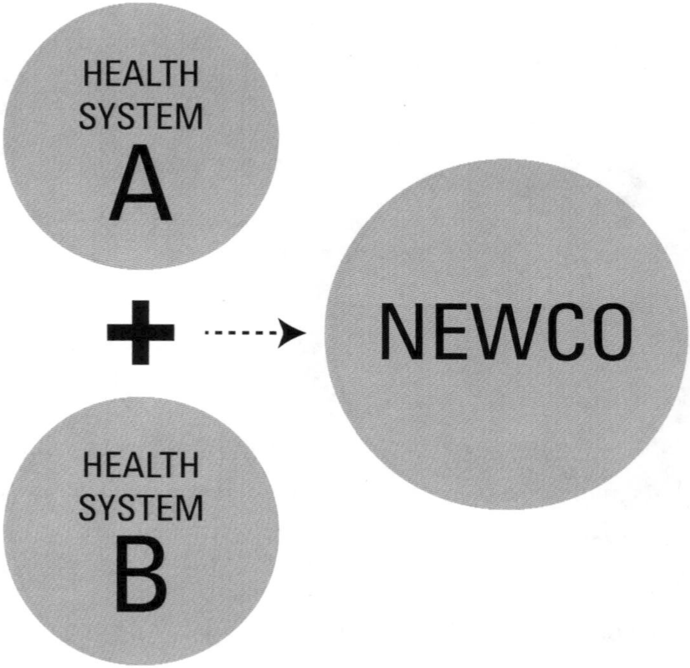

conversion: In a conversion, usually a not-for-profit hospital is acquired by an investor-owned hospital or company and changes (converts) its tax status to become a tax-paying hospital.

> A hospital conversion from a not-for-profit to an investor owned sometimes results in the creation of a new, independent community foundation. The foundation is created so that cash proceeds from the sale—the money left over after the hospital's debts and other claims are paid—can continue to support the community in a charitable fashion. A hospital conversion is usually given careful oversight by the state attorney general's office.

joint venture (JV): In a JV, ownership and sometimes control is shared. A common JV structure today is an 80/20 deal, where the acquiring hospital or company owns 80% of the hospital and the hospital itself retains 20% ownership. This structure can allow local hospital leaders to keep their hand in the direction of the hospital (which can benefit financially from its future success) while gaining a partner able to invest capital and expertise in the organization. Figure 4 shows a commonly used framework for a JV.

FIGURE 4
FRAMEWORK FOR A JOINT VENTURE

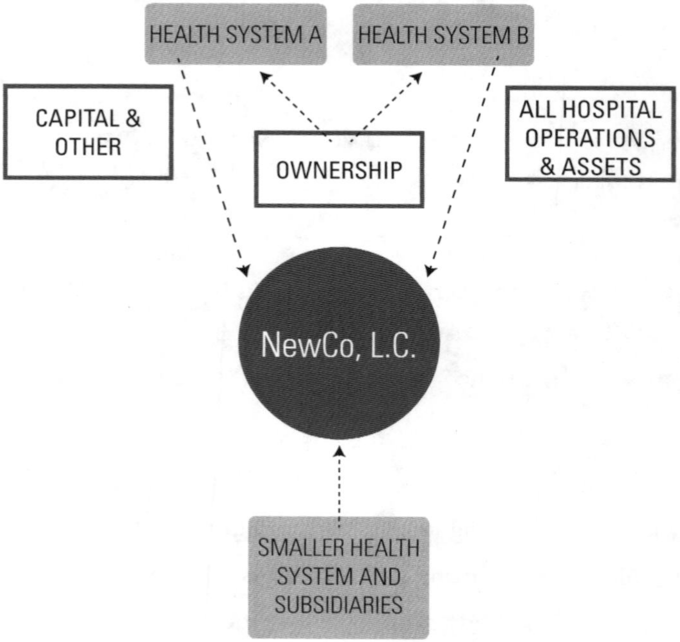

due diligence: This is the detective work an acquiring organization or company will conduct before finalizing any offer to invest in a hospital. It's like a house inspection before you take out a mortgage on your home. Due diligence can take many months and includes everything from inspections of the hospital's roof and parking lot to a deep dive into finances, legal matters, clinical outcomes, and more.

reverse due diligence: When a hospital is considering a specific partner or two, it will conduct its own detective work on them. This is likely to include visits by the trustees and leadership to hospitals currently operated by the potential partner as well as assurances of their financial strength, clinical capabilities, etc.

letter of intent (LOI): An LOI is usually the first agreement the potential partners will sign. The LOI is just what it says: It's a signal of intent or desire by both organizations to create a partnership together. Importantly, it does not mean a partnership will be created. Things can fall apart during due diligence.

LOIs are usually nonbinding, meaning neither party is bound or required to take the potential partnership any further. They usually include an agreement to negotiate exclusively with one potential partner. It's a sign that the "auction" to acquire or purchase a hospital has ended.

Most LOIs include a confidentiality agreement and a shared communications agreement, meaning both organizations agree to coordinate on all communications related to the potential partnership. This is important. It means you will be creating your partnership communications with another organization that will bring its own perspective and agenda to the conversation.

definitive agreement: The definitive agreement follows the LOI and due diligence. Unlike the LOI, the definitive agreement is usually binding. This document will reflect the true terms of the deal and signal the transaction is likely, pending government approval.

term sheet: Term sheets can be one page or 50 pages. A good term sheet will outline point by point the headlines of a transaction. Investment, control, commitments to charity care, commitments to employee benefits—it's all in the term sheet.

close: When the deal is closed, the transaction has been completed, the money has moved from one bank to another, and the keys have changed hands. An obvious semantic stumble to avoid: Be sure your message does not confuse the close of the *deal* with the close of the *hospital*. Anxious audiences often hear "close" and "hospital" in the same sentence and assume the worst.

Looking at these definitions on a macro level gives a picture of the level of integration you can typically expect as a result of the partnership. Figure 5 is a commonly accepted scale of integration that shows where each of these partnerships fall.

FIGURE 5

SPECTRUM OF PARTNERSHIP INTEGRATION

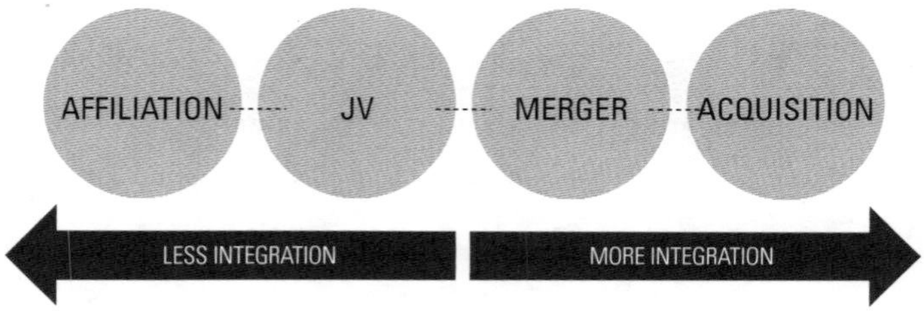

The Steps of a Partnership Transaction

Every hospital is different and every partnership is different, but the steps to completing a deal follow those of most major financial transactions.

Note that every milestone listed in the following six steps is not necessarily a communications event, but each is an opportunity—or a threat—for you to consider. They are:

- The partnership search
- Letter of intent
- Due dillegence
- Definitive agreement
- Regulatory approval
- Close

Depending on their communications strategies, some hospitals communicate early and often. Others wait until the definitive agreement has been signed. A few even wait until the deal is closed (not recommended).

While this list may look short, a partnership transaction can be a lengthy process. Deals can take from six to 18 months or more to complete. Use this structure as a foundation for your communications timeline.

Step 1: The partnership search

The board of directors or trustees decides to formally seek a partner to invest in or acquire their hospital or health system. They may hand-select a few favored potential partners or conduct a broad search for the highest bidder and strongest candidates. The search itself can take six months, a year, or more and can include some light due diligence, presentations by bidders, etc. Often, a broker is engaged to assist in the process and bring potential partners to the table for discussions.

While you may or may not choose to communicate that a search is under way, now is a good time to educate your key audiences on the need to change and evolve so your hospital can continue for years to come. It's really a time to create the context and set the table for the news.

Step 2: Letter of intent

The search is completed and an exclusive negotiating partner is selected. While the LOI is usually nonbinding and is not, in purely business terms, a substantial event, it is a major political event. It's a formal decision to negotiate with an expressed desire to partner. It lends momentum to the deal.

Step 3: Due diligence

True due diligence (and reverse due diligence) begins after the LOI is signed. This may or may not be an announceable event, depending on your strategy (and the leaky nature of your organization), but it's usually when the potential partner will walk the hospital halls, interview key physicians and staff, exchange information, and examine clinical operational systems.

It's worth noting that during the period between the LOI and the signing of the definitive agreement, there is frustratingly little "news" to announce. The issues on employees' minds—benefits, seniority, job security—cannot always be addressed because the matter is still being negotiated.

Step 4: Definitive agreement

This is a major milestone. The two organizations have come to terms and have agreed to enter into a partnership pending final government approvals or the resolution of key due diligence issues. Most potential partnerships are announced and publicly discussed at this point.

Step 5: Regulatory approval

State and federal regulatory approval can be a purely legal matter handled with appropriate paperwork ... or it can be a major political event that can blow up a deal.

Depending on the structure of the transaction, regulatory approvals can require testimony before your state's health department commissioners, public hearings before your state attorney general's office, certificate-of-need applications that include opposition from your competitors, and more. In addition, an in-market merger may catch the eye of the Federal Trade Commission, which will work to ensure the partnership is not anticompetitive.

> Knowing your regulatory environment is critical to building your communications plan. The words you use in your first announcement should be aimed at winning the regulatory approvals you need.

Step 6: Close

Ideally, this is a celebration: The partnership is secured. The future is defined (to some degree). While it's the end of the transaction, it's just the beginning of the new "you." In a sense, the real campaign is just beginning. We include an entire section—"It's Not Over When It's Over"—devoted to building this plan.

Figure 6 shows a sample timeline for completing each of the six steps.

FIGURE 6

TIMELINE FOR COMPLETING A PARTNERSHIP TRANSACTION

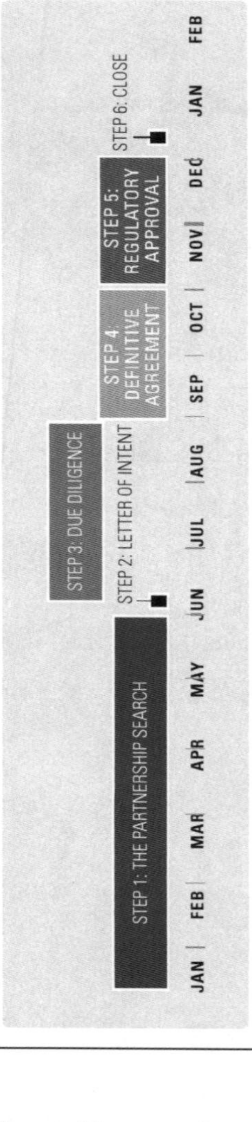

Partnerships Old and New

Let's pause for a moment from the details and steps of a deal, and look at the big picture. With this wide-angle lens view, risks and opportunities emerge that you as communicators must face.

Nashville is home to more than 350 healthcare companies, representing a $70 billion industry that impacts the delivery of patient care in every state. In a sense, it is our industry's capital.

At the core of Nashville's healthcare industry are several billion-dollar companies that own and operate hundreds of hospitals. Many have formed impressive partnerships with renowned medical centers such as Duke, Aurora Health, the Cleveland Clinic, and others.

Nonetheless, pay attention to the language these companies use today to describe themselves: They do not call themselves hospital companies. They are not in the "hospital business" anymore. Instead, they now own and operate "health systems."

Today, these organization are just as focused on developing "market density" and creating "vertical integration" in their existing locations as they are in acquiring new hospitals in new communities. Hospitals are just part of the equation.

In a sense, a Copernican revolution has come to our industry. Hospitals are being escorted out from the center of the healthcare solar system. Keeping patients away from the big box (instead of luring them inside) is the future.

In fact, the solar system itself is being replaced with a web of partnerships between providers of all stripes. It's a scramble to create a network big enough and interconnected enough to care for and promote the wellness of entire populations ... and make money doing it.

Accountable care organizations (ACO), clinically integrated networks, and risk-bearing bundles are just a few of the structural variations health systems are exploring to be prepared for the future.

To ensure they have the resources and scale to construct viable networks, healthcare leaders in every market are busy developing partnerships with independent physicians, physician groups, rehabilitation hospitals, ambulatory surgery centers (ASC), postacute care facilities, pharmacies, home health agencies, insurance organizations, and on and on.

The partnership race is on.

Risk and Opportunity Management

For communications leaders, each new partnership is an opportunity to exploit and a risk to be managed.

The rules and tools in this partnership guide are certainly applicable here as you move your system from being an organization that is hospital-centric to one that is network-centric (and, yes, always, always patient-centric).

Thinking holistically, politically, having a clearly articulated vision, making each partnership part of a larger narrative, and finding and equipping local advocates are vitally important as you grow your network.

Welcome your new partners in

Orient your new partners to you and your organization, even if you've worked with them for decades.

For your network to truly work, the sooner your new partner seamlessly connects with your organization, the faster you both will realize the value of the relationship clinically and financially.

Never assume they know what you need and expect from them. Tell them.

For example, consider creating a partnership communication package that expresses your issues and addresses their questions. Your package may include:

- Talking points about the partnership they can use with patients and vendors
- FAQs about your organization
- Logo and graphic standards for the partnership
- Media protocols and key telephone numbers

Consider conducting an orientation briefing with the new partner. During this, you'll want to conduct your own communications due diligence to learn how your new partner is (or is not) communicating with staff, patients, and the community. With that information, you can plan accordingly.

Importantly, as the communications leader, work to make sure others in your organization are also communicating with the new partner. Use your position to help facilitate the connections needed to draw the partnership together.

Expand yourself out

A new partner who carries and benefits from your brand is now responsible for delivering your experience.

Your organization has a "way": It's not merely a process or a logo, of course. It's a culture that offers a unique experience for patients and for staff and for physicians.

Your logo on the door carries a promise that the care delivered inside that office, within that clinic, or by that home health nurse will be of a certain quality, delivered in a certain way.

As your organization adds physician clinics or ASCs, your office will naturally make those services part of your overall marketing and communications program. The logos will change. The brochures will be edited. The website will be updated. All of that is important.

More important, however, is that you invest in educating the partner on your way of delivering the patient, staff, and physician experience demanded by your brand.

There is no more powerful marketing—for good or ill—than when a patient describes his or her experience with you. It overpowers all other communication investments. So invest heavily of your time and other resources to get the experience right quickly.

Change your language: A new kind of "we"

A network. Physicians. ASCs. Postacute care organizations. Outpatient centers. Clinics. Diagnostic centers. Emergency medical services. Health insurance companies. More than ever before, these critical pieces of our healthcare delivery system are being integrated, becoming one.

This means that the definition of "we" is rapidly changing.

That "we" now includes a more diverse set of employees. It includes a larger geographic footprint. It's an unprecedented blending of cultures, sponsors, backgrounds, and even faiths. It's the melding of former competitors. It's access for new patient populations.

> Your story for the future is critical—even more so than your quality rankings. Think about the traditional county hospital. It may have the highest patient-survey results, but if the folklore in the community is that it's the place for charity care, for massive trauma, or—worse yet—"you wouldn't send your dog there," then that is the story that will be told.

Thinking of yourself in terms of this new "we"—especially as you complete the partnership that prompted you to read this book—will change not only what you write and say, but also how you act and make decisions. It's a critical mental shift for this new era.

Tell your new story

This new "we" becomes your new story. Your brand. As communicators, we know that our story is the cornerstone to our identity.

As will be discussed in "Rule 2: Own the Message," as you lead your organization through any significant change, you must work to place the change in context of your vision—the place you and your leadership team believe your health system must go to be successful—while emphasizing those things that will not change—your mission and your values.

"We're adding these physicians to our team so we can become this ..."

"We're starting this ACO because, in the very near future, our patients and employers will need us to offer this ..."

"We're joint venturing with this rehab hospital so we can offer this seamless continuum of care here ..."

Take pains to explain the new partnership as part of a larger story that advances your organization toward a larger vision that fulfills its mission and the calling of its nurses, staff, and physicians.

Then celebrate these partnerships as they move the organization closer to the vision of its board and leadership. These steps can give your organization a sense of momentum and energy in a challenging time. Craft the vision that provides your health system a platform for putting your direction in a larger context.

Here's one example: Geisinger Health System is steeped in a rich, century-old history of care that began when its visionary founder, Abigail Geisinger, created a hospital in Danville, Pa., and instructed her first surgeon-in-chief to "make it the best."

That single hospital has evolved into one of the country's most widely recognized integrated health service organizations that includes a multi-specialty group practice, hospitals, and a 300,000-member health insurance plan. Its researchers are on the cutting edge of medicine, and its clinicians every day define what excellent care can be.

That strong founding vision to "make it the best," which is still often said around the halls at Geisinger, provides the organization with a strong historical context for its often-revolutionary and innovative approach to caring for the health and wellness of its communities.

A word on physicians

The smart healthcare systems that are truly thinking and working in an integrated way require communicating in a different way.

It shouldn't come as a surprise: Many of the rules that make up the heart of this guide apply to our new *we*, our new story, and our new industry culture.

The following are a few last thoughts on specifically integrating physician-hospital partnerships that can bring unique challenges. Let's dissect these:

- **Independent and referring physicians:** As hospitals employ more physicians, the remaining independent physicians need to be convinced, over and over again, that the hospital is evenhanded with them.

Independent physicians can see the millions of dollars that hospitals are spending to acquire physician practices and the ongoing expense of paying those salaries. It's not hard for these physicians to conclude the hospital will favor the employed physicians. This is a critical group because of the value they bring to the organization as an external partner, so a relationship with them must be cultivated.

- **Current employed physicians:** As the terms of the latest physician practice acquisition are shared through the medical staff, employed physicians need to hear from you to ensure they continue to feel valued and are informed how they fit into the changed lineup.
- **Employees affected by the acquisition:** Acquiring a large physician group practice can mean the hospital also has acquired some outpatient services, such as imaging or a lab that the practice operates. Special care needs to be taken to communicate what the acquisition of those services means for formerly competing hospital-based services. These new partnerships may introduce two kinds of employees in the same job: those who were part of the original system and those who are part of the newly acquired

organization. Everyone stays, in the best of cases, so what do they need to hear?

- **The community:** In competitive markets, some will see a group practice acquisition as an attempt to land a haymaker in the heavyweight fight between local hospitals. Many will accept that hospitals compete. Some will ask why the hospitals can't work together for the benefit of the community. Framing your story with the threat, the vision, and the solution—with the acquisition playing the role of the solution—can help neutralize that sentiment. (Discussed in "Rule 2: Own the Message.")

Communicating a Partnership

Navigating change is nothing new for hospital communicators. Change is our normal. Regularly, we tackle shifting federal regulations, competitive pressures, and swiftly evolving communication tools.

However, a partnership discussion elevates all of this usual, day-to-day work and adds emotional, political, operational, and financial elements to the mix. You are left with what can only be described as one thing: change management on steroids.

How to Think About Partnership Communication

Traditionally, hospital leadership deal teams have a laser focus on the financial, operational, regulatory, and clinical elements of the transaction. That makes sense, of course.

But, as communicators, we know that a hospital partnership is much more than the numbers and rules and charts. It's more than the timelines and the deal terms outlined and previously defined.

A hospital partnership is an emotional, political event in the life of an organization. In fact, a transaction that makes financial, operational, and clinical sense can die a quick death if it doesn't make political sense to a community or cultural sense inside the walls of the hospital.

> According to a recent *HealthLeaders Media Intelligence Report, M&A: Hospitals Take Control,* culture clash was the No. 1 deal-killer—above political considerations, access to capital, and integration issues. Want to see more? Purchase *Intelligence Reports* annually by going to *www.healthleadersmedia.com.*

You know the unique and powerful emotional connection people have with your hospital. Your nurses fulfill a mission through their care for their patients and for each other. Your physicians have an emotional and economic relationship to your hospital that's vital to their livelihood and your success. Your patients and their families experience life-changing events inside your doors: *My son was born there. My mother died here.* The sense of ownership can be strong: *It's my hospital.* The emotions your patients and staff feel are powerful political forces.

This can all work for you (or decidedly against you) as you lead your organization toward a new future. Managing these political forces is at the heart of your work as hospital communicators.

In a time of change, the cost of ignoring the value of communications is high. The plans of your trustees and leadership to sell or buy or partner can be squashed if the message—your story—is not well-crafted or delivered in the right way by the right people at the right time.

Done correctly, a well-orchestrated, assertive campaign can energize your team, excite your patients, and discourage competition. It puts your political strength to work for you and your organization when you need it most.

A partnership is a defining moment for an organization, whether it plays the role of buyer or seller. It defines your calendar: All things will have occurred before or after the partnership. It is a holistic event: Everything and everyone matters because everything and everyone is impacted.

It is, in short, a big deal that will capture the attention of your key audiences and place your organization and your leadership on stage under a very bright spotlight.

Success in this hothouse environment requires relentless and comprehensive communication.

Throughout the transaction, the key audiences for both organizations must be engaged assertively, steadily, and as transparently as possible, using a variety of communications tools (existing tools, social media, press, personal interaction, etc.) with a smart and consistent core message that advances the cause and counters objections.

> There are many tools that can be used together to create a unified message. These are noted in "Rule 8: Overcommunicate." In addition, because it is so critical, we outline a full-fledged and stand-alone website development plan for a partnership. Creating a public hub of information like this is a key tool that matches the tone of the entire partnership itself: Be transparent, be accessible, treat the partnership like a momentous occasion and a game-changer for your organization. All of this can be found in "The Power of Digital Media" in Section 3.

It's not just advertising or press releases or a Twitter feed or a special event, though the work may include all or none of these. Those are just tools, after all. A different way to approach this work is to think of partnership communications as a political campaign to be waged and won. The political campaign analogy captures the comprehensive and intense work that successful partnerships need.

Your Political Campaign

Politics, in the sense of campaigns and candidates, is not everyone's favorite subject. However, the analogy does provide an evergreen framework with which many are familiar. There is a clear goal: to win the day.

The point is that your hospital is embarking on an initiative that is unusual and beyond the daily experience of most operators. If the political analogy does not work for you, find one that helps you think differently. After all, you have a candidate to run, a platform to build, a diverse population with varying agendas to sway, supporters to mobilize, opposition to neutralize, and votes to win.

Every successful political campaign has a crystal-clear goal: to win the most votes on Election Day.

To get there, good campaigns run a tightly disciplined communication effort that mobilizes, unites, and focuses a host of resources toward the single goal of winning.

That's your task, too.

How does this translate to hospital and health system transactions? Let's talk about the fundamentals, which are also outlined in Figure 7.

FIGURE 7

THE KEYS TO WINNING YOUR CAMPAIGN

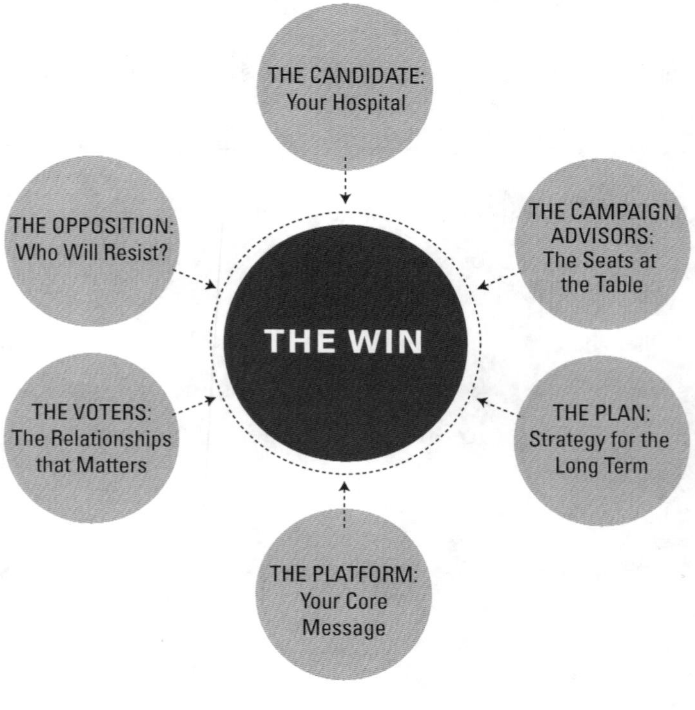

The candidate: Your hospital

Your organization is the candidate in the transaction "election," and your most trusted leaders personalize the campaign. These leaders must be active, visible players throughout the effort. You won't win this campaign relying solely on the marketing "remote control" of paid media and email blasts. People follow people, after all, not buildings or brands. (This is discussed in "Rule 5: The Messenger Is a Message.")

Most importantly, your board and leadership team must be fully engaged. You are leveraging your hard-earned reputation and spending political capital in a very public initiative. Commitment to the campaign is fundamental to success.

The campaign advisors: The seats at the table

Every successful transaction campaign has a cabinet, a focused group of six to eight advisors who represent all aspects of the transaction: the money, the clinicians, the politics, the regulatory issues, the media, etc. Working together, this team informs your campaign and shapes it over time. One team, one plan.

This may be a true team that meets regularly, or it may be the role you as the communications head take on in a more one-on-one fashion. Regardless of the structure, the point is to make sure you are asking the right questions and gleaning the information you need from all corners of the deal and all of the key decision-makers. Then, bring that information together to create a whole picture and a complete and cohesive message. (This is discussed in "Rule 1: Get Smart. Stay Smart.")

The platform: Your core message

Now is the time to define your organization, what it stands for, and its concrete vision for the future. You must transform the technical benefits of the deal—all that information you learned and continue to learn from the deal team members—into a platform of driving motives and deal benefits that matters to an entire community.

What matters most politically and culturally for making this transaction a success? What do people need to hear, and what would be nice for them to hear? Campaigns drive action: What action do you need your audience to take to help you?

This is your platform and the rallying cry that can turn your stakeholders into advocates and neutralize the opposition. This is your core message that will pull your audiences through change. (This is discussed in "Rule 2: Own the Message.")

The voters: The relationship that matters

Relationships are key to ensuring a successful transition. Period.

Who supports, who opposes, and who remains on the sidelines can make or break a deal. Case in point: An angry group of offended physicians can stop a major hospital transaction in its tracks.

Dissect your audiences and create highly targeted plans for each group that can influence your success.

Start with your internal advocates: nurses, frontline staff, and physicians who carry enormous credibility in the community. If they're against your deal, you've got an uphill battle to wage. If they appreciate and support the campaign, you have powerful advocates you can mobilize. (This is discussed in "Rule 6: Get the Talk Right Inside, Then Out.")

The opposition: Who will resist?

Every meaningful campaign has opposition. A hospital transaction is disruptive. It changes the playing field and is likely to put someone at a disadvantage.

There's your in-market competition, of course. They may take great interest in your plans and do whatever is necessary to publicly (or quietly) derail your plans ... or just recruit your best physicians and nurses while the transaction is under way.

But opposition may come from inside your walls, as well: legacy issues between old rivals, spats between warring physicians, the natural fear of the disruption and uncertainty caused by change that can lead to passive and not-so-passive resistance.

Of course, elected officials, media, and others may join in as well. This is where candlelight vigils to "save" a hospital are born.

Expect resistance, plan for it, and quickly engage when it comes calling. (This is discussed in "Rule 4: Think Like the Opposition.")

The plan: Strategy for the long term

This is a campaign, not a news flash. It occurs over time. It begins before the initial announcement and steadily continues beyond the conclusion of the transaction. Your hospital transaction campaign will likely take many months of steady activity.

Build your campaign from the first announcement with the conclusion in mind.

Hospitals have tremendous political power that can be tapped when needed. The key is to think politically and strategically, and use this guide to help your organization leverage that strength to win what may be your hospital's most important strategic goal. This post-announcement campaign is discussed "It's Not Over When It's Over" in Section 3.

The Case for Communications: Take It From a Matchmaker

It's one thing to listen to the words of communications experts on why it's critical to have top-notch communications at the table during a hospital partnership process.

It's a completely different experience to hear similar advice from top hospital transaction advisors, whose role is to inform and guide systems and hospitals at the outset of partnership discussions and through transaction execution, from start to finish. They think through all of the possible mechanics of partnership arrangements and consider high-quality communications to be among the top elements that make a partnership proceed smoothly to completion.

So we take a break from our own advice and offer that of Anu Singh, senior vice president with Kaufman Hall. Singh brings many years of experience as part of Kaufman Hall's Strategic Options and Mergers, Acquisitions, and Partnerships practices, working exclusively with hospital leaders as they assess partnership options, identify the best-fit partner, create a win-win partnership structure, guide the organizations through the due diligence and final evaluation process, and negotiate, finalize, and close transactions in a way that sets up the new entity (or entities) for success.

Author: How should any leadership team—and especially a communications leader—think about the period they are about to enter? Certainly, it will be a lot of work in operations, logistics, and financial considerations, but what type of emotional or political elements describe the situation best?

Singh: Hospitals considering partnering with another hospital, in any form of collaboration, place their organization and its key stakeholders in a highly visible position.

The creation, vetting, and execution of a clear and cohesive set of communications are key, whether the hospital is financially challenged or is partnering from a position of strength. Preparing an organization for a transformative move requires evaluating its prospects and challenges and knowing what can be shared appropriately publicly and how to do so. Without the public understanding of the organization's current position, it will be harder to articulate and potentially execute the vision for the future.

Author: Big picture: What is the first step of partnership considerations?

Singh: Set clear objectives. This task is likely the most important component conducted by the board and senior management team in the strategic partnership process.

The objectives define the business goals against which prospective partnership options will be evaluated, as well as why such pursuits are more attractive than stand alone or other options. They also provide the framework for the governing transaction documents. Covering such topics as strategic plans, clinical programs, capital and facility commitments, physician and employee commitments, community goals, and governance considerations, these objectives often become the shared values and vision of the two organizations.

That's where the communications portion comes in: It is important that these objectives are communicated clearly and thoroughly from start to finish.

Author: In this book, the idea of assembling a campaign team, or at the very least, charging the communications leader with keeping an open line of communication with all key players in the arrangement is critical. Who are those key players? How do you ensure representation of each perspective when evaluating and securing a partnership arrangement?

Singh: Kaufman Hall brings together a small group of key decision-makers whose work will speed and facilitate the partnership exploration and transaction processes. This team typically includes senior management, financial and legal advisors, a small task force of board members, and individuals with communications expertise. Often, the communications expert will be outside counsel who works with the organization's existing staff and a local public relations firm.

This team is best assembled soon after discussions arise within the board about partnership—and long before a partner is chosen. These advisors and senior management typically manage the day-to-day details, while the board task force measures and tracks performance against relationship objectives, provides critical advice on the development of the transaction, and reports to the full board at defined milestone stages in the process.

Author: So what specific role does a communications expert play in the eyes of someone more focused on the workings of the transaction?

Singh: Communications team members should be involved in all stages of ongoing project oversight. They help to inform, evaluate, and make communications recommendations to the management/advisory team and board task force, and manage the development of information specific to key audiences. When appropriate, the experts also develop a contingency communication plan in the event of unexpected information disclosure.

Author: How would you describe the tone of the kinds of communications that are most effective?

Singh: To ensure a uniform understanding among all stakeholders, education is a key element of the communications process.

Education-based communications involve not only informing the board and leadership team about how the partnership process works but also communicating with internal and external audiences the benefits of the partnership to the community, to the organization, and to each individual. Success in such communications will help set a path for a smooth partnering process.

Author: Who are the audiences you recommend paying attention to?

Singh: Constituent groups that should be considered within a communications plan include:

- Staff
- Physicians
- Other clinicians
- Unions
- Donors
- Partners/affiliates
- Patients
- The community
- Elected and regulatory officials
- Government bodies
- Civic and political leaders
- News media
- Rating agencies

Author: When is the best time to start to communicate?

Singh: In advance of initiating the partnership process, communications with key audiences beyond the management and board decision group generally is very limited and high level. However, every transaction is unique and the nature, timing, and scope of the communication plan are specific to the organization and its situation.

Often, the communications team works collaboratively with the hospital's internal resources as well as local external communications specialists to develop a communication plan specific to each key audience.

Author: Why do partnerships fail before they get to the closing stage? When they fail, how should it be handled?

Singh: A lack of understanding of the partnership process, guiding objectives, and general expectations of the partnership is often at the root of failed or delayed transactions.

Serious issues can surface during the due diligence phase, which is the time when both parties ensure that no issues exist that would impact willingness to consummate the transaction or to keep the same financial offer or commitment and identify any issues or risks that require further investigation. It is critical that the task force and leadership teams fully understand the importance of frequent, responsible communications with key audiences during this time.

The level of stakeholder scrutiny on the prospective transaction will be at a level rarely experienced by the organization in daily operations.

Author: What makes a partnership successful? Right price? Right "synergies" in operations?

Singh: The success of a hospital partnership hinges on the acceptance and participation of stakeholders, including the community, hospital staff, and employed and independent physicians. Stakeholders need to understand the benefits of pursuing a partnership, as well as the ways in which a partnership ensures the viability and growth of healthcare in the community going forward. Experts should develop and implement the communications plans to achieve such buy-in throughout the process of identifying and securing a best-fit partner to meet community health needs into the future.

Author: What are some pointers on gaining such buy-in?

Singh: A thoughtful consensus-building process brings stakeholders on board. This process typically includes:

- A communications plan that engages with each constituent group at appropriate times during the partnership process

- Clear, consistent communications that maintain discipline from the time of announcement of a letter of intent between two organizations through the transaction closing; this can take many months, so discipline is critical
- Ensuring that stakeholder expectations are realistic and practical, and hence can be communicated to appropriate stakeholders
- Making it a goal to achieve a partnership that brings key constituent objectives into a singularly shared vision, not to simply get a transaction done

Author: Any closing thoughts?

Singh: The right set of advisors is key and, given the substantial amount and magnitude of change in the hospital industry, choosing firms with extensive, deep, and varied expertise is critical.

Section 2

THE 10 RULES OF ENGAGEMENT

Rule 1: Get Smart. Stay Smart.

THE BIG IDEA

- ✦ Comprehensive interaction is the foundation for building your campaign.
- ✦ Understanding and utilizing many perspectives is invaluable to building your message.
- ✦ Ask and answer every question: the easy ones and the not-so-easy ones.

Take Action: Be a Reporter

Information is power. As the communications officer for your healthcare organization, you know that building an effective and persuasive message—not to mention a winning campaign—requires a complete and current understanding of what is happening, when, where, and why. But it's not just the facts you need, of course. You need to build and manage the political dynamic, the flow of events, and key decisions that will drive the creation of the strategy. Then, once you understand what is going to happen and why, it's time to anticipate how others in your hospital and your community will respond to it.

Understanding Perspectives—Fast

How do you dissect, understand, and predict your stakeholders' response? How do you do so quickly?

Imagine you have joined a political campaign as the communications director. When you sit down for your first strategy session, you join a crowded table. There's the fundraiser, the scheduler, the policy analyst, the pollster, the grassroots get-out-the-vote director, the speechwriter, the volunteer coordinator, the event planner, the candidate ... and you.

The perspectives of each of these individuals may differ widely. On a given issue, media experts will respond one way, political audiences another, volunteers another, and so on. Yet all of these have to be calculated together to create a single, focused, winning strategy.

To have a winning campaign, information must flow freely. Every effort and idea must point toward a single goal and fit with the others like a puzzle to create a unified front.

Now, think about the campaign you have to run: Whose perspective do you want—need—at your hospital to inform your planning? No one source has it all. You have to look at a variety of sources for the facts and the insight that will make your plan smart and savvy. A few suggestions:

- **Administrative leadership.** This will likely be the CEO or his or her designee. The CEO is the natural go-to source for big-picture information: What is the vision for the new partnership? What are the terms of the deal? You'll need insight into the board-level discussions.
- **Internal legal counsel (and outside transaction counsel, if any).** Legal counsel can walk you through the legalities of the partnership and, importantly, the regulatory approval process the transaction will require.
- **Financial advisor.** An in-depth look at the financial terms of the deal is key. An outside broker (if the hospital has engaged a broker to lead transaction negotiations) should be able to give you national perspective on the transaction and its context in terms of other partnership activities occurring around the country. It's likely he or she will also have some unique insights into the other hospitals or hospital companies in play.

- **Government relations.** Your government relations officer, lobbyist, or consultant can offer insight into how local and state elected officials will respond to the news, and how their reaction may help (or harm) your regulatory approval process.
- **Clinical leadership.** This is someone who knows your physicians and nurses well. In any partnership discussion, the physicians matter. A lot. The nurses also matter. They are not just a key audience; they are powerful communicators. Understanding how they are (or are not) impacted by the transaction is key. If you are the buyer, an understanding of the physician and nursing community in your potential partner is just as important. Stay close to these leaders.

Your work with these individuals should be an ongoing conversation. One meeting will not be enough. The information will change, sometimes dramatically, as the partnership search and negotiations progress. Draw from them all again and again as you move through the campaign.

Creating a Campaign Team

In an ideal world, your interactions with these individuals will not be isolated events. They will be ongoing and stem from regular, scheduled conversations where each member is physically at the table.

This is your campaign team. Again, like a political campaign, this is the team that comes together regularly—even daily in the heat of a campaign—to create, assess, and adjust strategy and message.

They act together: One team. One strategy.

The benefit of the team is that you are able to ask all the questions that need to be asked in one room, and craft answers and actions knowing how they impact all of your key constituencies. It's a critical advantage.

A few additional benefits:

- **Consensus:** This team will work together to develop the initial communications plan. While you lead that creation, getting team members' input throughout means that the final plan is based on consensus and bears no surprises.

- **Coordination:** A team coordinates constantly throughout the campaign's weeks and months. Coordination will become increasingly challenging as you near the close of the deal. You will save a lot of stress and back-and-forth legwork with a regularly scheduled time to meet, and with a team that feels it's moving together.

- **Resilience:** This give-and-take helps keep your team in control of the message and hedges against knee-jerk reactions to a roadblock and against missing an opportunity without the fullest context of the situation. Surprises will occur during partnership discussions. A team that meets regularly is more likely to anticipate problems and less likely to react poorly.

A Virtual Campaign Team: Communication's Role

Of course, building a physical campaign team is not always possible. Internal politics, time constraints, and sheer geography may get in the way.

When that happens, create a virtual team. Designate the leaders you need to tap, maintain your plan, and let each individual know he or she is part of your virtual campaign team. Then talk to each team member. Ask questions. Share perspectives. Make the message work together.

Day one is too late; start asking questions now

Your detective work begins well before the first public discussion of any partnership transaction.

In an ideal scenario, you will have begun your work 90 to 120 days prior to the beginning of a formal partnership search by your board (if you are a seller) and 90 days before you pursue a partnership with another (if you are a buyer).

At the first whiff of a planned sale or purchase, go through the list of questions in the next section, "Take Action." You may not be in the inner circle of these big decisions yet, but it will do your organization a world of good to begin preparations.

> Bringing communications into the loop is often not the top priority for C-suite leadership or the hospital transaction team, but it's critical. At the first inkling that something may unfold, talk with your CEO or project leader to present a case for the role of communications in supporting the action of the board and protecting the assets of the hospital. Note: For reasons of confidentiality, only you may be briefed. You may have to keep this information to yourself for a certain period, but the time gained in that span is invaluable.

Take Action: Be a Reporter

Information is power. Use the following questions to spur your reporter-like inquiry for the facts and insights you'll use to build your communications strategy.

- What is the vision for the partnership?
  - How does it fit a broader narrative about our organization?
  - How does this help us fulfill our mission?
  - Are we entering into this partnership because of financial pressure? How so?
  - Are there tangible benefits we can articulate? An investment in specific technology or service lines?
  - In general, what stays the same—and what changes?
- What is the transaction process?
  - What stage are we in: Letter of interest? Definitive agreement? Due diligence?
  - What regulatory approvals will we need?

- When will we have specific information for employees?
- What is the timeline for the process?
- Who must approve this transaction on our behalf? On behalf of the potential partner?
- Will our or their physicians be part of the decision-making process?

- What are the terms of the transaction?
  - Is there an up-front payment? If so, how much?
  - Will the hospital require a conversion from not-for-profit to investor-owned or from Catholic to non-Catholic affiliation? (This is discussed "Troubleshooting: What to Do When ...." in Section 3.)
  - Will a foundation (if a not-for-profit hospital is converted) be created as a result?
  - Is there a commitment to invest capital? How much?
  - Will there be an assumption of debt? If so, how much?

  - How does governance and control change?
  - Are there commitments to employees? What are they?
  - Is there a commitment to continue charity care at a certain level?
- What kind of partnership is being considered? A joint venture? A merger? An acquisition?
  - What are the benefits of this structure?
- How will this news be received?
  - By physicians?
  - By nurses and staff?
  - By community leaders and elected officials?
  - By patients and their families?
- Will there be resistance?
  - From where do we expect resistance?
  - Why?
- What about communications?
  - When can I speak with my counterpart at our potential partner? Who is the point person?

- Have any decisions been made about communications to date?
- Are our communications restricted for any reason?

Rule 2: Own the Message

THE BIG IDEA

- ✦Lead with your vision; use the partnership to support it.
- ✦Build your message in three phases: threat, vision, and solution.
- ✦Emotion is key to your message.
- ✦Never, ever, *ever* forget the patient.

Take Action: Create Your Core Message

A hospital partnership is complicated. Your core message can't be.

A transaction can be frightening. Your core message must inspire confidence.

A deal can stir poisonous cynicism. Your core message must be credible and candid.

A partnership can make your best people doubt. Your core message must rally them to the future you see.

Tall order, right?

Here's the messaging challenge: A hospital partnership is an exceptionally complex and multilayered undertaking. Human resources, clinical, financial, regulatory, IT, and a host of arcane matters are evaluated and negotiated as any deal comes together.

It's easy to think these details are the core of your message. But they are not. These are the gears that make the watch work. They are interesting and important. But, first, people want to know the time.

Your challenge is to tear away the clutter to form a partnership message that is simple, clear, and compelling.

Getting to the Core

It begins with your core message.

Your core message is the communications platform. It sets the tone, the themes, and the key word choices—the very language—for communicating the details of the partnership. All your communications tools, including talking points, scripts, releases, and FAQs, will be based on your core.

Building the core is hard work. At its heart is the vision that is driving your partnership. The core message must paint an enticing picture of the post-deal future. It must be bigger than the terms of the deal. It must be trustworthy. And it must bring together the perspectives discussed when asking all of the questions covered in Rule 1: Get Smart. Stay Smart.

There are plenty of data points to be communicated: money, employee retention, services to be added (or cut), physician politics, issues of governance and control, etc. These are important matters, to be sure, but don't get lost in them. These details are secondary and complementary to the themes you'll need to use to sell the partnership.

Classic change management messaging is an excellent foundation for communicating a partnership. Instead of details, this messaging structure tells a story and builds a reason to support the message.

There are three elements:

- Threat
- Vision
- Solution

Figure 8 shows how these three elements affect your core message. Let's walk through each in order, because each is built off the previous element.

Threat

For an organization to accept substantial change, its people must believe its current situation is untenable. They must believe that staying with the status quo will be ultimately harmful to themselves, their patients, and their mission.

FIGURE 8

ELEMENTS OF CHANGE MANAGEMENT MESSAGING

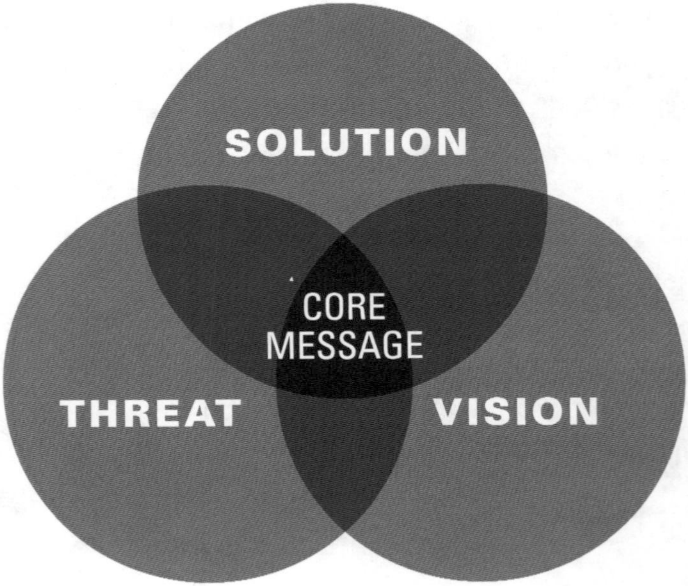

This threat may come from pressing financial troubles or overwhelming competition. But it can also be anticipatory: Looking ahead, we see that our hospital must evolve to remain competitive. The world is changing; we must change with it to continue our service, to continue to be a leader.

The threat is not necessarily a distress flare. It can be a signal of leadership and a recognition that the organization must change to meet the challenges of the future.

Be sure, though, that the threat is credible. Too often, hospital leaders refuse to share their hospital's real challenges—its financial struggles, for example—and are then baffled when their staff and physicians won't accept the need for change.

When thinking about the threat, consider the following so that you can build a solid case for change:

- What is it about the hospital's situation that makes this partnership necessary?
- Is competition a factor?
- What financial challenges do we face?
- What impact does healthcare reform have on our need for change?

- Are reimbursements declining to the point that we need a new source of funding?
- What happens if our hospital does not complete this partnership?
- Is the partnership preferred or is it necessary?
- Can we survive without it? For how long?
- Would we search for another partner if this transaction is not completed?
- What data do we have to help paint a picture of this threat?
  - Patient volume?
  - Reimbursements?
  - Competitive analysis?
  - National or regional trends?

Remember, acknowledging any of these challenges as a true threat to your organization is not a sign of weakness. Every hospital in the nation is facing one or more of these threats.

It's a signal of leadership that your organization acknowledges the challenge; it also positions the C-suite as a true

Although not specifically pertaining to mergers and acquisitions, hospitals across the nation named the following as their greatest threats in *HealthLeaders Media 2013 Industry Survey*:

1. Reduced reimbursements
2. Physician shortages
3. Organized labor
4. Healthcare reform
5. Industry consolidation

More threats, opportunities, and comments on outlooks can be found in a free download of the *HealthLeaders Media 2013 Industry Survey* at the HealthLeaders website, *www.healthleadersmedia.com/breakthroughs/257025/Hospital-Merger-and-Acquisition-Strategies*.

leadership team that is taking action to ensure the organization and its people have a future.

Vision

This is the picture—presented as concretely as possible—of what the future can be if the partnership is successful. "This is the destination where we are headed once the challenges and the threat are managed and conquered." It's what the puzzle looks like when all the pieces come together.

This may be a story about scale and market share, or the wedding of complementary services, or infrastructure improvements. It may be a story about repositioning the entire enterprise to remain competitive and strong.

Importantly, this vision must have two parts to be compelling: the big picture of who you are as an organization, and the close-up look at how life will be better for your nurses, physicians, and patients going forward.

The vision must be operational, aspirational, and community-based, touching on all of the following questions:

- What will the combined organizations look like?
- What happens to leadership and who is at the helm?
- What will the delivery of healthcare look like in five years and 10 years, and how does this vision support that?
- Does the organization's mission change?
- How is the "new" organization better or different for staff, physicians, and patients?
- What is the long-term role of staff in this partnership? The role of physicians? Other staff?
- What does the new partner uniquely bring to the table?

- How does this new combined organization address the threats we face?

On announcement day, you will not know every detail, and that's okay. However, it will be necessary to know the overall picture so that your nurses, patients, physicians, and community leaders understand what you are all working toward—together.

Solution

With the threat and the vision established, the partnership then becomes the vehicle to get you from where you are to where you need to be.

Said another way, the transaction is not the goal; the transaction is a tactic to help your hospital tackle threats and fulfill its strategic vision.

In messaging the solution, describe what will change and, just as important, describe what will not change. Among your staff and physicians, the fear of instability can conjure dramatic (and often negative) scenarios of what is about to happen within the halls of your hospital. Head these issues off at the pass with as much clarity as possible.

Additionally, address the day-to-day impact of the partnership. You may not know the details on announcement day, but when you do, share them. This includes employee retention and compensation, benefits, retirement, paid time off, pensions, insurance, reporting hierarchy, etc. For your staff and even your physicians, the core message is as important as the broader issues of governance and investment. Your staff members won't fully embrace your big picture core message until they are comfortable that their personal stability is assured. Similarly, physicians—whether employed or not—need to know the positions of their colleagues with whom they serve patients are secure.

You have likely answered a lot of these questions in your initial research, because they really are the root questions to ask. But it's worth making sure that you have covered your bases as far as logistics so that you can turn these very operational next steps into a vehicle with momentum to achieve that vision:

- What are the key components of the deal?
- How are the cultures of the two organizations similar? How are they different?

- What should staff and physicians do and expect between today's announcement and the conclusion of the deal?
- When can staff and the community expect updated information?

What Matters Most in a Core Message

To reiterate: It's not the details that matter most. It's the politics, the message, and the heart of what's happening that can lead to the success or failure of a deal.

You cannot sell a hospital partnership with a spreadsheet, a discussion of your bond rating, or debt relief. Financial deal points may be crucial facts, but they must support a broader emotional message that speaks to your organization, your mission, and the calling of your nurses and physicians.

But at the same time, don't ignore these facts. Debt relief matters because it allows us to invest in our people and upgrade our facility so that we can fulfill our mission of service. Align them so they support your bigger goal.

When the possibility of instability is raised—when a potential partnership is announced—this question dominates:

What's in it for me? Job security, benefits, wages, paid time off, etc., will be the first things that will come to mind when you announce this transaction. In fact, staff, physicians, and others will find it difficult to hear your core message about furthering the organization until they are assured of their and their teams' job security.

In the early stages of a transaction, you may have only a few of the answers, if any. Make it clear you are thinking of this diligently, and give staff a sense of when they can expect answers. Ensure that whatever you say sounds like you. You are already introducing a new way of life to your organization through the partnership. Bring familiarity to the news with a tone that matches who you have been. The alternative would be to deliver the partnership news in controlled lawyer-speak. That change of tone can also be seen as a message, and not a positive one.

Announce and communicate a partnership together as the seller and the buyer—issue one press release, common talking points, common FAQs, joint letters, etc. Consistency of message, so everyone in both organizations is hearing the same message and the same answers to critical questions, can be the first public demonstration of how the partnership itself is going to be. Make your communications a working model of the future.

A word on promises: Do not make promises or provide assurances that you cannot keep. If you know a layoff will follow the conclusion of the deal, don't promise that everyone will have a job. Those games will deeply damage the organization for years after a partnership is completed.

Take Action: Build Your Core Message

Now, build your core message based on the information, perspectives, and thoughts given to you by the people you interviewed who have answers. Start by organizing them into the three elements of a good message: threat, vision, and solution.

It may help, too, to think about what you want your top three takeaways to be when someone hears your message for the first time. These are the points that, no matter the conversation, make the lasting impression. They should closely follow the threat, vision, solution structure, but should be boiled down and plain-spoken.

It may help to create these three takeaways first, so that you can guide the remainder of your messaging. Or you may find it's easier to compile all the messages and then whittle them down into the top points.

Ultimately, your goal is this:

- Threat
  - Point 1: Statement that something needs to change
  - Point 2: What about the organization or the environment makes this so?
  - Point 3: How does the organization fit in the broader community/national context?
  - Point 4: What will happen if change doesn't occur?
  - Key takeaway
  - Sample core message: Change is coming to every hospital in the United States. The question isn't if; it's when and how that change will occur. We recognize that our organization must change to continue our mission and service to our patients

and community in the face of the evolving healthcare environment.

> It's worth a reminder here: Never, ever, ever forget the patient in your vision and solution.

- Vision
  - Point 1: What must the future organization become?
  - Point 2: Who are the key players involved?
  - Point 3: Why is this the right goal (versus others considered)?
  - Point 4: What main benefit does it bring, including what stays the same and what changes?
  - Point 5: How does it ensure security for the hospital, the staff, and the patients?
  - Key takeaway
  - Sample core message: We will be part of a new organization that will be better positioned to care for our community. Our priority is to provide excellent, quality care, a high value for our patients, extraordinary service, and expanded access for all who need it. Ultimately,

we will be better equipped and have the resources to continue our mission for years to come.

- Solution
  - Point 1: How will this partnership take the organization where it needs to be?
  - Point 2: What can we expect in the next 90 days?
  - Point 3: What role do employees/physicians play? How can they help?
  - Point 4: How are jobs, benefits, privileges, etc., impacted?
  - Point 5: How can people get more information?
  - Key takeaway
  - Sample Core message: This partnership means that we will work together to ensure patients have a more coordinated care experience here at our hospital, as well as access to additional care. Our caregivers will work with one another, physicians will join forces, and patients will have more opportunities at new locations. While there may be some changes, we anticipate that this partnership will mean more excellent care.

Rule 3: Be Transparent

THE BIG IDEA

- There are no secrets.
- It's not a matter of *if* you should be transparent. It's a matter of *when* your information will be public.
- Being the active source of information can help you stay in control of your message, even when you have to be vulnerable about the challenges of a partnership.
- Your leadership team must be committed to transparency.

Take Action: Ask the Tough Questions

"A lie can travel half way around the world while the truth is putting on its shoes." That's pre-Facebook, pre-Internet, pre–mobile phone—even pre-telephone—wisdom from Mark Twain.

Now, a lie can travel around the world three times and appear on CNN before the truth can pick up its smartphone to tweet.

Today's technology enables a lightning-fast, unfiltered flow of information, however credible or vetted it may be. It also has shaped us to expect that not only will important news be shared, but that we'll engage in a dialogue about it.

This means one thing: The issue of transparency is not whether news about a transaction will be shared. It will be. It's too hot and dramatically affects the lives of too many people to sit quietly in your boardroom waiting for you to pull back the curtain.

The issue really is whether your leadership will guide the sharing or be overrun by it. This is a question of risk management, credibility, and message control.

The Risk of Secrecy

Of course, leadership teams and boards like to hold strategic information close. It's understandable. Information is power and leverage in negotiating a hospital transaction. What's more, the potential of a transaction, either to buy or sell, can be disruptive, distracting, and even damaging to an organization. Who wants that?

But the risk of secrecy can also be high. A leak of inaccurate or incomplete information can threaten leadership's credibility and place the organization in a reactive, rumor-killing campaign that eclipses your core message. Deals fall apart when the wrong people get half-baked information.

The Opportunity of Transparency

Communications leaders have the opportunity to educate the deal team on the importance of transparency, calling out the benefits of being transparent as well as the risks associated with secrecy.

> Being transparent means delivering your message first to the audiences that matter most to you. It does not mean sharing sensitive or confidential information or every detail about the potential transaction. It means sharing what you can—in broad terms, early on—and being candid about what you cannot share today.

Organizations that take this approach enjoy these advantages:

- **You set the stage.** By being first, you are able to define the terms of the conversation—why a transaction is necessary and what leadership hopes to accomplish through it. You are able to discuss what the transaction is and is not. All reactions are based on the terms you've established. This is the foundation of message control.

- **You establish yourself as the trusted, credible voice.** By being first, you assume the position of authority and confirm leadership as the place for staff, physicians, and the community to look for credible information about the transaction. (Note: The rumor mill often has more credibility than leadership. It takes work to earn this credibility.)
- **You are empowered to engage in dialogue about the deal.** Taking the lead frees yourself and your leadership team to talk with staff and others about the potential of the transaction.
- **You weaken the detractors.** By being first, you subvert forces that might work to undermine you and your organization by using leaks, half-truths, and misinformation against you. By being transparent, you take away from your opponents and competitors their very big stick.
- **You confine the conversation.** It's counterintuitive, but by being first, you define what you can and cannot talk about today, and you earn the credibility to limit the discussion until a later time. You can now set

milestones for when the next round of information will be available.

Transparency is a fundamental strategic decision that is the foundation of your communications strategy. Own it to control the message and lead the conversation in your hospital and your community. At the same time, commitment to transparency *reduces* but doesn't *eliminate* the challenge.

To be clear: Transparency is valuable, but it does not by itself make the transaction rosy and care-free.

A hospital transaction is a disruptive event in the best of circumstances. Even when the result will be genuinely positive for everyone, it's scary (particularly in a shaky economy). Fear is a powerful emotion. By being actively transparent, you and your leadership can greatly reduce the anxiety associated with a transaction, but it's unlikely you will eliminate it.

Transparency starts with your leadership team—the board and the C-suite. From there, transparency extends to the entire campaign team, that small group of trusted advisors you draw on to create a core message and develop and execute your overall communications strategy. If team members are not transparent among themselves and with you, you cannot do your job.

Take Action: Ask the Tough Questions

Transparency is so essential to a successful transition that it should be the first commitment your leadership team makes. When you are transparent—when you share information and don't hide under your desk from your public—your focus stays sharp, and your team is energized and equipped.

Now's the time to ask and answer the hardest questions honestly and candidly as a team.

You won't answer every one of these questions in your first discussions, but by asking the difficult questions and identifying the tough issues, you begin to take away others' negative power. The tough stuff becomes not questions to ignore, but problems to solve. This opens the door to communicating even the most challenging issues.

Questions the sellers should ask themselves:

- Are we willing to be transparent with our staff and physicians?
- Is our potential partner willing to be transparent?

- Will our leadership team survive the partnership transaction?
- Will we keep our name? Our culture?
- Will there be staff layoffs or services closed because of the partnership?
- If the acquirer is a Catholic hospital, will we adopt Catholic directives regarding women's services? If we are a Catholic hospital, will services at the hospital change?
- Does our potential partner have a reputation that is better or worse than ours?
- Does our potential partner respect us? Does it want this partnership or is its hand being forced?
- Among our staff, who will report to whom when the partnership is completed?
- Among our physicians, who will be most threatened when this partnership is completed? Can that threat to them be addressed?
- Is our board and leadership team united in this direction? Is the potential partner's? How will we manage divisiveness?

- What criteria has the board used to select a partner? Did it have outside counsel, such as a healthcare consultant or transaction attorney?
- Will our board keep key issues confidential? Will the potential partner's? If there's a risk that it won't, can we address the board?

Questions the buyers should ask themselves:

- Why is this hospital a good fit for our organization?
- How will we invest? For how long? How much?
- What reputational issues with the new hospital will we have to overcome?
- Are there unions that are part of the new hospital? How will we deal with them? What are the legal parameters?
- Will we honor the purchased hospital's charity care policy?
- What challenges from the federal or state governments might limit our ability to make a hard decision?

WHAT TO DO WHEN LEADERSHIP SAYS THEY DO NOT NEED A COMMUNICATIONS CAMPAIGN

Josh Nemzoff is president and CEO of Nemzoff & Company, LLC, and has guided not-for-profit hospital boards and leaders through hundreds of transactions over the last 30 years. In these three decades, Nemzoff's work has spanned the country, representing more than $10 billion worth of transactions. The following is a few thoughts from Nemzoff on how he approaches transaction communications in his work, and how he responds to occasional resistance from board members and hospital leaders.

Having worked on nearly 300 hospital merger and acquisition transactions, there is not really much that I have not seen.

When we approach the work, we always use a project team and tell our clients that the team consists of three people: the project director (which is our role), an experienced transaction attorney to cover the legal issues, and a really good crisis/communications counselor. The communication counselor may be an in-house expert experienced at this work, or a specialist consultant engaged just for this project. We almost always make that recommendation in a board meeting, and the question that comes back 90% of the time is "why do we need a crisis/communications counselor?" Our response is, "because if you are thinking of selling your hospital, you are about to have a crisis." This answer is often met with resistance. Below are the common pushback responses we hear, and how we address them:

WHAT TO DO WHEN LEADERSHIP SAYS THEY DO NOT NEED A COMMUNICATIONS CAMPAIGN (CONT.)

We want to keep this confidential

Yes, we are sure you do, but there is no way a buyer can perform due diligence and not have it leak. It is going to leak. Count on it. Plan for it.

Our board knows how to keep a secret

Really? Maybe. However, we have never seen a board keep a deal secret, and your board will not be the first. It will leak. Again, count on it. Plan for it.

We don't want to upset the employees and the medical staff

Then don't do a transaction. They will be a lot more upset when they read about it in the newspaper. They are going to be even more upset if they think you are hiding something. Transactions are tough enough. Surprising your people with news of a transaction is explosive. That alone can blow up the deal.

We have a non-disclosure agreement, so we are not allowed to talk about the deal

You do not need to talk about the deal. You need to explain that there is a deal and why there is a deal. By the time the reporter calls you, it is too late.

WHAT TO DO WHEN LEADERSHIP SAYS THEY DO NOT NEED A COMMUNICATIONS CAMPAIGN (CONT.)

The local reporter is not savvy about hospital issues and does not like us

Then don't talk to him and let all of the people who are opposed to you give their side of the story. Then the reporter will make up something that he thinks is your position. Don't let your emotions get in the way. Without your active participation, there is less than a 20% chance that the reporter will get it right.

It's only a non-binding letter of intent; we are going to wait until we have something concrete

Only one out of a hundred people will have any idea that an LOI is a non-binding document. The headline on your LOI will be "community hospital is sold." Get in front of it. Buying and selling a hospital is a difficult process. If you do not have an experienced communications counselor and a comprehensive communications campaign, you are running the risk of getting slaughtered in the press, in social media, in your community, and in the hallways of your hospital.

For every deal that gets closed, there are at least two that fail because the board and leadership got cold feet–unprepared for the political games, unequipped with effective messages, and unsteady when the opposition came calling.

Rule 4: Think Like the Opposition

THE BIG IDEA

- ✦ Anticipate your opposition: their goals and their tactics.
- ✦ Engage the resistance—don't retreat.
- ✦ Neutrality from detractors is a win.

Take Action: Plan for Opposition

Every hospital partnership transaction has opposition. Every one.

Opposition to a hospital transaction can range from the passive-aggressive resistance of staff to offended physicians shifting their referrals, to a communitywide candlelight vigil orchestrated by an outraged mayor. It can be fed by your competition or the media or community groups or even from within the walls of your hospital. It can be loud, but often it is very quiet.

Consider these few flavors:

- **Stealthy and quiet:** This is the heart of the rumor mill. These are the whispered conversations that undermine leadership. It may come from employees, residents, local elected officials, you name it. It stems from the general fear of the unknown and of change that threatens security. This kind of resistance grows when there is little information and much speculation.
- **Listen to me, I just want to know:** This type of challenger raises his or her hand in a meeting and asks questions that sound like opposition but are truly a plea for information and a desire to have a voice. The intent here is not to derail the deal—not yet, at least—but certainly to get answers now. Address these challengers quickly, and you can turn them into supporters. You may not agree on every point or have all the information they want today—you probably won't, in fact—but you can make them part of the conversation. Ignore them at your own risk.
- **The power play:** This is the overt, loud, intentional kind of opposition that uses a public forum as a stage from which to advance its agenda.

For example, your physicians may send patients to the neighboring competitor to signal their discontent, or threaten to open an ambulatory surgery center across the street. Community members may rally at the town hall, collect signatures on petitions, hold vigils, and call elected officials and the media to draw attention.

Labor unions, too, are sensitive to these moments of change. If their concerns are not addressed, informational pickets can be very effective weapons for getting your attention.

Some of these opponents may be softened and turned into advocates with effective communications and relationship building. Others, however, will fundamentally and unswervingly disagree with the partnership and must be neutralized or sidelined for the partnership to be successful.

A note on opposition from competitors: In an in-market merger, it can be the back-door sniping across campuses that lets you know just how hard this culture shift is going to be.

Your competitors may work hard to recruit your nurses, physicians, and other caregivers. They'll play on their fear of the unknown to persuade them to jump ship ... and, for extra fun, they'll tell the media that people are fleeing your hospital because you're too focused on the dollars and cents.

Defuse Opposition Through Engagement

Most opposition can be softened through engagement. By engagement, this means personal interaction in a conversation about the strategic direction for your hospital. This is not about emails or even snail mail. It's about eye-to-eye, face-to-face conversations.

Resistance can stem from people's very human desires to be secure and have a voice in the significant events that affect their lives. Acknowledge that desire and speak to it by creating opportunities for dialogue about the partnership transaction.

Your leadership team should be in continual conversation with your staff, physicians, board, and community leaders as you move through partnership discussions. Not in the "I ran into the mayor at Rotary" manner of bump-and-run contacts, but through deliberate and planned conversations with people who matter. In a political campaign, they run daily tracking polls to keep a finger on the pulse of the electorate. These planned conversations can do the same for you.

Create opportunities for dialogue: town halls, forums, online chat rooms, small group conversations with physicians, your state legislative delegation, you name it. Don't be afraid of bad news; invite it in so you can address it head-on. Identify the people who matter—who can help or hurt your partnership—and seek them out.

Don't underestimate the power of social media. Civic clubs and printed newspapers are not the only places people engage in conversations, though they certainly top the list of influential communication vehicles. Entire mergers between hundred-million-dollar organizations have been knocked down by concerned citizens who organized and gained traction within a matter of hours or days through social media. Be there, too, listening, learning, engaging. See "The Power of Digital Media" in Section 3.

Don't back down

> Work with your leadership team members to identify contact lists and engage friends as well as enemies. Build a grid of who on your team will talk to whom, how, when, and how often. Then report back and compare notes. Where are the opportunities and what rumors need to be squashed?

Engaging with an audience does not mean appeasing the audience. It's unlikely you'll be able to answer every question your nurses ask. It's also unlikely that they'll like every answer you give them.

The goal of engagement is to show your respect by listening, demonstrating that you recognize the emotional element of the event, and strengthening your credibility by investing your time and intellect in the conversation. There's a reason politicians do "listening tours" as they launch new policy initiatives. Model that.

Remember, some opponents simply can't be turned into supporters. Do not invest your time and energy into winning the unwinnable. Your competition will most likely fit into this category. Anticipate their pushback, surround them with your supporters, and move on.

Take Action: Plan for Opposition

By introducing a hospital partnership, you are advocating what might be an earth-shaking event in the life of your organization. Expect resistance. Plan for it, in fact.

If you've anticipated resistance, you won't be shocked when it comes. Instead of stewing, you'll be acting.

Ask yourself the following questions when you plan to manage resistance. And remember, don't underestimate your opposition's potential to cross the line from logical to irrational concern.

1. Points of group resistance

   Who may oppose and what could be their issue? Consider each group carefully.

   - Internal:
     - Nurses
     - Staff
     - Managers
     - Off-site staff such as skilled nursing facility, home care, or lab staff
     - Other staff
       - Housekeepers
       - Food services employees
       - Call center staffers
     - Physicians
       - Employed physicians
       - Independent physicians
       - Large physician groups
       - Joint venture partners

  - Volunteers
  - Foundation board of directors and donors
    - Divisive board members
  - Organized labor
- External:
  - Payers
  - Large employers
  - Local, state-elected officials
  - Regulators
  - Media
  - Competition
  - Community/advocacy groups
  - Religious leadership

2. Points of individual resistance

   Using the list above, identify any individuals who may be naturally resistant to the partnership you are exploring. Ask yourself what individuals may lose influence or money because of the partnership.

3. Plan for each

For each group and individual, anticipate what this group or that individual may do or say in opposition to the partnership. Ask yourself these questions:

- What will their issue(s) be?
- How are they likely to express their resistance? By writing a letter to the editor? By moving patients to another hospital? By sowing dissent within the halls of the hospital?
- What is our best response to each issue? What is the core message these groups or individuals need to hear? How can we weave these answers into our overall messaging?
- Who is the most credible person to engage each group or individual?
- Who are the potential advocates that are influential to each group or individual?
- How willing are we to engage each group or individual in conversation?

Rule 5: The Messenger Is a Message

THE BIG IDEA

- ✦ Your message is more than your words.
- ✦ Who speaks is a message in and of itself.
- ✦ How they deliver the message matters.
- ✦ It often takes a team approach.
- ✦ Trust is the most critical characteristic of your message.

Take Action: Build Your Spokes-Team

Who is the most trusted leader in your organization?

It may be the CEO—that's the go-to answer—but this may be the wrong answer.

It's an important question because when announcing something this important, the messenger is a message.

Who communicates important information is as important as the information itself, and is key to shaping how news is received. For news this big, don't assign the spokesperson role out of habit; make the assignment part of your strategic communications planning.

Attributes of the Right Spokesperson

The goal, remember, is to win universal confidence in your core message: the reason why the partnership is necessary and the vision and solution that creates a new way forward for your organization.

The goal is not, however, to win a beauty pageant for a specific leader, board member, or physician.

Your leading voice—your spokesperson—should embody trust and confidence. Not everyone who hears the news about the partnership may like what they hear, but they should trust the information and the intent behind it.

The person who can do this may be your CEO. But for the sake of your organization, be candid in your planning: If, for whatever reason, your CEO is not trusted or known within your hospital, use somebody else who is. Borrow his or her credibility. Use your board chair, chief medical officer, chief operating officer, or chief nursing officer. It's that important.

One person may not have the trust and confidence of every single audience. It may take a team of spokespeople. There are many important audiences to talk to over many months. For a significant partnership announcement, you will need multiple spokespeople.

Having a "spokes-team" helps you spread the word faster with a chorus of supporting voices. It strongly signals a broader endorsement of the partnership when multiple advocates fan out through the organization and the community to make your case.

A spokes-team also gives you the flexibility to connect the right supporter with the right audience.

For example, your CEO might be quoted in the release, interviewed by local media, and speak at the town hall meetings. But the chief medical officer who has built relationships with key physicians over the years may be the best point of contact for your physicians. Your board chair may know only a few people within the hospital, but he or she may be the best representative to engage your mayor or state legislative delegation.

Formal or informal, these supportive voices only further your goal. Now is the time to catalogue and leverage all your (and their) relationships.

Some unlikely candidates

Knowing the qualities, consider these often-overlooked spokespersons or advocates:

- **White coat.** He or she may not be involved in operations like a CEO or chief operating officer, but a white-coated chief medical officer, a leading physician, or your chief nursing officer can carry credibility that a "suit" cannot. It's harder to question the statements of a confident caregiver.
- **Patient advocate.** Beyond your board (which is an excellent place to mine for advocates, of course), an independent community leader who has also been a patient can be a powerful resource. These individuals offer third-party endorsement based on the very crux of the issue: continued access to high-quality patient care.
- **Elected official.** You may think that a politician will not be supportive, but your partnership may offer the candidate/incumbent a platform for demonstrating how he or she is making a difference in the

community's delivery of healthcare. Do not be afraid to ask if the politics are right.

Equipping your Spokesperson

It's unlikely that your spokespeople have been hired for their communications style. They may be a medical or quality expert, or hang an MBA diploma on the wall, but they will still need your help in preparing to take on the challenge of communicating the deal.

Equip them.

Your spokes-team will need tools and must know how to use them. These are likely to include one page (no more) of talking points, an extensive document full of the questions and answers that must be consistently communicated, and, possibly, a slide deck to help them walk through a conversation discussing the partnership. It may also be important to arm them with a process for handling (or not handling) media inquiries well. Not only do these tools make your advocates more comfortable, they also help you ensure consistency of message.

Train your advocates to listen as well as speak. Each conversation is a mini-focus group where new concerns and questions may be raised. Be sure your spokes-team members share what they are hearing "in the field." That information can be invaluable to you as your communications campaign unfolds.

> Train your spokespeople. Ensure they are ready for anything from a one-on-one at the grocery store to a more planned question-and-answer session. Your designated media spokesperson will need special preparation, too. Use your Q&A document and the answers you have already sought in the first sections of this book.

Take Action: Build Your Spokes-Team

Identifying your spokes-team is a matter of connecting dots: One dot represents the key audiences that can help (and hurt) the development of the partnership. The other dot represents the individuals who can be capable advocates for you and who are trusted by those specific audiences.

Remember: Who delivers your message is just as important as the message they are delivering.

A few questions to ask:

- Do they have trusted relationships with an audience that matters to your hospital?
- Can they deliver a message consistently? Will they stay "on message?"
- Are they confident and calm under fire?
- Are they accessible, personal, and approachable for the audience?
- Will they overtly bring their own agenda to these discussions?
- Will they offer feedback?
- Can they be trusted with confidential information? Can they keep a secret?
- Are they supportive (or likely to be supportive) of the transaction?

Rule 6: Get the Talk Right Inside, Then Out

THE BIG IDEA

- Physicians and nurses have power and credibility. What they say matters.
- Talk to your internal audiences first and often.
- Turn your audiences into advocates.

Take Action: Build Your Audience Lists

It's the moment of truth.

Your hospital leadership has just announced its decision to partner with the big academic health system down the road. The talking points are good. The media covered the story well.

Then this happens: At the grocery store the day after the announcement, a former patient walks up to one of your hospital's nurses and asks, "What do you think?"

What the nurse says next makes all the difference.

Words of support from the nurse can be empowering and assuring. Words of distrust, anger, or fear can be poisonous. They can harm the deal.

Patients Trust Physicians and Nurses

Why is that conversation so influential? Because your nurses and physicians have far more credibility than you, your leadership, your letters to the community, your advertising, or your website.

There's a reason we put caregivers on our billboards and in our TV commercials. They are deeply trusted and rightfully considered healthcare "insiders." It's where people go to get the real scoop.

Over the many months of a transaction, your physicians and nurses—in fact, every one of your employees—will have countless conversations with patients and community leaders at your hospitals, in their examination rooms, at the grocery store, at church, at home, over the backyard fence—everywhere. What they say matters.

Your internal audience—your physicians, your nurses, and all your employees—is your primary audience. It's the group that has to support you before you can ever win the hearts and minds of your external community.

Said in another way, it's vital that you get the talk right inside your hospital first.

The Best Internal Conversations

A few tips:

- **Break down the audiences.** We often broadly discuss nurses and physicians as if they are a homogenous group. You know they aren't. Your specialists may have concerns not shared by your primary care physicians. Your obstetric nurses have a culture unto themselves. The emergency department cowboys need to be wrangled. Your managers and directors are both an audience and an important group of day-to-day messengers. In short, it's not one-size-fits-all. Invest the time to develop a core message and tactics that speak to each group.

- **Don't let them read the headline first.** You know this, but it's worth repeating: Your employees should hear about the potential partnership before anyone else. Before they read about it on the newspaper's website. Before they get a call from a competitor saying, "Come work over here with us."

- **Give them tools.** When you share the news, equip your physicians and staff with tools to share with others. Help them capture your vision and your solution so they can describe it to others. Acknowledge that they are powerful voices—they know they are—and ask for their help in advancing your hospital.

> Once you start to communicate with your internal audiences, confidentiality is out the door. Remember that each of your communications to your internal audiences should be phrased in a way that you are comfortable seeing in the newspaper. Especially in an age of social media, employees will forward memos to the newspaper, tweet about the news, or even call the paper to come on over to the hospital for the day's latest scoop. Reporters even have direct access to staff through friends and neighbors.

Take Action: Build Your Audience Lists

So first things first: Build your list and get detailed about it. Who matters to you internally and externally? We talk about external list building now because it's important when we get to the next rule on advocates. For each group, be sure to make a few notes as to what they will want to hear most, what their greatest concerns will be, and how they best receive information.

As you gather info for Rule 1: Get Smart. Stay Smart., build these lists. Make sure your lists are current—phone numbers, email and street addresses, as well as correct titles—so that as you get closer to announcement day, you are focused only on the message and not on getting an email address for the mayor. Then, assign the right spokesperson to reach out to each individual. Potential lists include:

- Internal
  - Board
  - Leadership
    - C-suite/administration
    - Management staff
    - Directors
  - Staff
    - Nurses and other caregivers
    - All others

  - Physicians
    - Community/contracted
    - Employed
  - Volunteers
  - Auxilians
  - Foundation board members
  - Community board members
- External
  - Patients
  - Media
    - Local papers
    - National papers
    - Trade publications
    - Wire services
    - Radio
    - Television
    - Blogs and online sources
  - Elected officials

    - Local
    - State
    - National
- Community leaders
    - Aligned organizations
    - Competitors
    - Business owners
    - Other movers and shakers
- Religious leaders
- Vendors
- Large donors
- Labor unions
- Regulatory authorities (who may already be in the know)

Rule 7: An Army of Advocates

THE BIG IDEA

- ✦ A team of advocates is like having an extra set of eyes, ears, and hands.
- ✦ Your best communicators and leaders may not be on your payroll.
- ✦ Give them clear action items, but also a little license to act.
- ✦ Listen to their input and give them feedback.
- ✦ When needed, organize them into a classic, political grassroots–style group.

Take Action: Build a Grassroots Team

In the thick of your partnership communications campaign, the to-do list is longer than you can handle alone: Run the plan. Tweak the messages. Draft the memo. Update the website. Call the reporter. And on and on. It's the nature of an active campaign.

You need help. You need a team of advocates who are empowered to be ambassadors for your campaign; advocates who can take the important messages out of the hospital walls and bring important information back to you. These are individuals who can take your communications goals—and all of your planned, strategized, buttoned-up, and vetted materials—and provide a third-party, credible human angle that your organization and spokespeople simply cannot. Your advocates can elicit and share feedback from the community that you want to hear—whether you like it or not.

By activating these advocates and, if needed, organizing them into a classic grassroots team, you expand your resources far beyond what you, your department, your spokes-team, or internal audiences can do alone. Said another way: It's time to call in the troops.

> In Rule 6, we talked about getting the talk right inside. Yes, there will be advocates inside, and your communications plan will reach them regularly. However, Rule 7 focuses on individuals outside of your organization who will benefit from a similar amount of attention so that they can mobilize in your favor.

Advocates in Action: Today and Tomorrow

Your advocates can accomplish the following:

- **Boost your organization's reputation when it matters most.** Reputation is key. It is vital to your organization's long-term success. Your external advocates are critical to your reputation. Their support—along with your physicians, staff, and nurses' continued good work and positive attitudes—can combine in a way that your opposition will find hard to fight. What each of these individuals says at the grocery store, at church, and among friends makes a difference in who seeks care at your hospital. If they talk positively about you today, and can endorse your partnership, your reputation only gets stronger.
- **Add third-party credibility.** You can do all the award-winning advertising and marketing in the world, but your community members' support adds an element of credibility that no amount of money can buy. Most people ask friends and coworkers for recommendations when seeking a hospital or physician—they will do the same with your merger and acquisition campaign. Word-of-mouth marketing is the most powerful marketing you can generate.

- **Give people a job.** In a time as emotional as this, your supporters will want a way to be involved and speak up. They will create their own outlet, so why not help shape that? For your supporters who have more time to devote, this could be the role of monitoring and commenting on social media sites in your favor. You may ask them to write an op-ed for the local Sunday paper with the highest readership. You may simply ask them to have conversations, listen to the feedback, and bring back what they hear so that it informs your campaign strategy. Developing mini-plans like this gives your supporters a goal.
- **Neutralize your opposition.** Your advocates in action can cause even those who are disinterested or who disagree with your efforts to feel the pressure of a groundswell of support.

Energize Your Advocates

You probably already know many of your natural supporters. Now you need to pick the best and turn them into advocates.

Individuals' titles can certainly carry weight in convincing others to support your deal, but their personal credibility also matters. As you think about the advocates you can recruit, consider who those individuals are and how they are regarded in the community. They may not have a noteworthy title, but their informal credibility can speak even louder.

Your advocates must be trustworthy. Community members must hear advocates' words as believable and heartfelt, so that when they utter your messages, there's no question as to their support.

Similarly, if you are going to ask them to listen to feedback in the community, you have to be able to trust that they will deal with that feedback appropriately and share it honestly with you—even news that may be hard for you to swallow.

Loyalty matters, too. Someone who has been a patient at your hospital and has a good story to tell will be an even stronger advocate than those who simply support the deal but visit a competitor for their care.

Lastly, be sure your advocates represent a diverse cross-section of your community. Everyone may read the op-ed written by your mayor, but they may trust only those to whom they are closest. Identify advocates in the business community, the not-for-profit community, schoolteachers and educators, and advocates in the religious communities. This is similar to how your hospital leadership builds your board—with varying perspectives that matter to the livelihood of the hospital.

You will find these people in your own circles, but you may also want to tap other leaders in the organization who are closer to certain audiences. For example, the Chamber of Commerce president might know of a good business leader.

Approaching Your Advocates

Being an advocate is a personal, emotional choice. Approach your potential advocates respectfully and personally. Your first step is a conversation. Said another way, advocacy-building work is more than an email campaign.

Tell potential advocates why you want to meet and sit down with them face to face. Any meeting is beneficial, from 10 minutes in their office to an extended lunch. Affirm the traits you value in them and why you need them solidly in your corner. Talk through your threat, vision, and solution messaging and listen carefully to their reaction.

Next, ask for their advice. Specifically:

- How would you get this message out?
- Who needs to hear this?
- What questions will people ask?

Listen to their answers. Then ask for their help, and give them clear guidance when they agree to advocate for your facility, such as:

- Please share this message in as many conversations as you can.
- After you have these conversations, please call me. I'd love to hear—candidly—how they went.
- If you are willing, consider writing a letter to the editor of our community paper, being active on social media, or holding a meeting among influential friends and colleagues to share your support.

Set a time to reconnect. Then, above all, thank them for their time.

If possible, bring your advocates together in a mini-focus group to discuss what they've heard.

When Advocates Become a Grassroots Group

Sometimes you need more than what individual advocates can do for you. You may find it necessary or advantageous to formally organize this team.

A team of advocates is known as "grassroots" supporters, and this team can be a powerful force. Grassroots organization takes coordination on the front end, but it can take on a life of its own once it's up and running.

These individuals are listening and acting on your behalf—bringing them together as a group gives you the benefit of their thoughts, ideas, and feedback in an interactive setting. We look at this work in three stages, based on having already worked with advocates on an individual level.

Phase 1: Formation and intelligence gathering

In the beginning, your grassroots group may be most valuable when you use them as extra eyes and ears, just as you did when they were individual advocates. The individuals who make up your team—five to 10 people is a good number—can learn things that no one else will tell you. They understand the culture outside administration offices. This intel is invaluable, and there's no other source for it. Ask what feedback they are hearing, either individually or by bringing these individuals together as a group.

As your grassroots team members work on your behalf, continue to affirm their critical role in your campaign. After all, they are taking time out of their own day and putting their own reputations on the line for your cause.

Phase 2: Public efforts

As the partnership campaign continues to progress, your grassroots team will identify ways to transition from its listening efforts to outward communication that is more vocal and public. Your team will start to think of the work as a coordinated effort.

Suggest three to five tasks that team members might choose to do together and provide ideas on how they can complete these tasks. It could be a group editorial written to the newspaper about the benefits of the partnership as seen through the eyes of the community. Or it could be a supportive rally the night before the papers are signed. Some of the most active grassroots groups will actually create a slogan, a logo, and collateral material.

As your group builds its plan, your role as the hospital's lead communicator—whose job it would be to organize these efforts among internal advocates—is to guide and then take a step back. It might be uncomfortable at first, but giving these individuals freedom will help them own their work. Consider offering them the following supportive efforts:

- Encourage them to seek out more members once the plan is in place and the group has its end goal in sight.
- Offer the chance for members to speak to the hospital CEO or ask the CEO to speak to critical audiences and endorse the work of the grassroots team.
- Give financial support to some of the collateral materials or plans. For example, you can pay for buttons with a slogan or logo or purchase the ad space needed for an advertorial in a publication.
- Celebrate and endorse your team's wins as they happen. These victories can be as small as adding team members, as well as celebrating announcement day or completing the paperwork for the deal.

Phase 3: Postpartnership reputation building

Your grassroots team can live on as an extension of your new normal campaign that is outlined in "It's Not Over When It's Over" in Section 3.

This postpartnership work begins with the most public and celebratory phase of the grassroots work. Whereas the first two phases had goals that ended on the day the partnership became formal, the goals now shift toward culture-building, creating a new way forward, and defining what this newly created entity is.

Giving Your Grassroots Group License

When you have assembled your team, let team members go—supported, but not led, by you or your leadership—to share their thoughts in their own way. They may get a fact wrong or be a little too loud, but they will get a reaction from the community that you won't get on your own.

You might say, "This is too dangerous. In an effort that requires such coordination as a partnership campaign, we can't afford a misstep."

Your external audiences—and your employees, for that matter—already have that freedom. They are already out there talking about the hospital. So give them a framework for what to say, support them, and then let them add their own flavor.

Take Action: Create Your Grassroots Team

We've just talked about the theory of a grassroots team. Now let's go back and talk about how to get each of the three phases up and running when you are building that interactive grassroots team:

Phase 1: Formation and intelligence gathering

Plant the seed.

- To kick-start the effort, bring together six to eight trusted advocates for a focus group discussion. Talk about:
  - Their thoughts on the partnership
  - What strengths they and their colleagues see
  - What barriers or challenges are being discussed
  - What rumors they hear in the community
  - How they can help

- During this discussion, ask them to continue to listen for this feedback and report it back to the team.
- Include a communications leader from the hospital in this discussion as a moderator.

Empower the team.

- This cannot be overemphasized. These individuals must feel that they have the freedom to take action as they see fit.
- Your role is to share the information you have about the partnership, raise any challenges that the group can help overcome, listen to their thoughts, and then tell them how you can support whatever plan they develop.

Create and structure the group.

- The group may choose to formally organize itself, select leaders, and set a clear definition for success. At this stage, that can be a simple decision to meet and share feedback to determine what needs a response.
- The group may create its own name and slogan.
- The group may agree to meet weekly to accomplish this work.

Phase 2: The plan

Build the plan.

- This begins with dreaming: No idea is off the table.
- Adapt the campaign messaging to a more grassroots feel.
- Then comes the practical work of schedules, work plans, point persons, event planning, and the like. Put it to paper.

Execute the plan.

- The best-laid plans feature:
  - Minimal involvement of administration
  - Advocate-led initiatives

Phase 3: Postannouncement action

This could be a good time for your internal grassroots team to meld with your efforts in the days, weeks, and months after the partnership is finalized. It may include:

- Rallies and initiative launches
- Celebrations of partnership goals achieved
- Meet-and-greets among employees

- Internal posters that show staff members from each entity working together
- T-shirts or stickers

Rule 8: Overcommunicate

THE BIG IDEA

- ✦ People are hungry for assurance and conversation, even if you can't give them details.
- ✦ Make information as accessible as possible.
- ✦ Develop a suite of communication vehicles.
- ✦ It's not over when it's over.

Take Action: Create Coordinated Communications Vehicles

You cannot communicate too much in a time of dramatic change.

In fact, there is a rule in communications called the "seven times" rule. It's simply this: Most audiences must be exposed to a message seven times before they really hear it for the first time.

For communicators, this means that by the time you're tired of saying the same core message over and over, people are finally hearing it.

Have you had the CEO say, "Haven't we said this already? We need to say something new." That's when people are just hearing it.

"Me First" Communications

In change-management communications, it's important to know that when someone believes their world is being turned upside down, they absorb information in stages, closely following Maslow's hierarchy of needs. For example:

1. They want to hear that they and their families are "safe," and that their livelihood and their benefits are secure.

2. Then, they will want to know that their colleagues are safe and that they'll be able to continue their patient care mission.

3. Only then, with those assurances in place, will they be ready to hear your core message about how the partnership is good for the hospital and for the community.

If you cannot offer these personal assurances, getting your internal audiences to care about your strategic vision can be a challenge.

To be clear: Healthcare professionals are practical people. They may want (but don't necessarily expect) guarantees of employment for life. Who has that today? They understand you cannot have every answer to every question on day one. But they are hungry for assurance and conversation, and will require it before they can become supporters. The old cliché is true: They want to know that you care before they care about what you know. You show that care by talking to, visiting with, and engaging them. Be present for them.

You get the point: In a time of change you must communicate—a lot—to stay in control of your message.

A Competition for Attention

Look at your email inbox. How many unread messages do you have? Our bet is many. Some probably even have that little red exclamation point indicating a high priority next to them. Think hard about the many mediums you will need to employ to ensure that your core message sinks in.

Some of your key audiences will require a personal conversation before they hear you. Others may require a billboard or the daily check of a website. For some, a memo is much more effective than a speech. And then there is the idea that staff will not believe anything until they hear it from their peers.

Consider these four effective tactical approaches:

- **A weekly message.** At a minimum, communicate with your staff and physicians every week about the progress of the partnership transaction. Communicate even if there has been no substantial progress. This drumbeat of messages kills rumors ("The deal is dead!" "The deal is about to close!" "They're firing us all!") and helps you maintain your position as the voice of authority for the transaction. This message can come from your key spokesperson and be as brief as a paragraph or longer if there are updates to report.
- **Name the campaign.** Giving a graphic identity to the campaign that is specifically for the length of the partnership is an effective step, especially for hospitals or healthcare systems with a host of initiatives under way. By doing this, you can make your updates stand out from the clutter. This can be as simple as pairing the two organizations' logos side by side with a word

or slogan (e.g., Care for Our Community: A Future for Our Hospital).

- **Launch a partnership website.** Build a stand-alone website that is unique to the partnership transaction. These are public sites accessible to all, with statements, hand-selected FAQs, videos of leadership, a collection of news coverage, letters from leadership, etc. It's also a place where anyone can ask a question and get a moderated answer. These sites become 24/7 centers of information that staff, media, lawmakers, and others turn to for facts about the transaction.

- **Create opportunities for dialogue.** You're talking a lot to—or at—employees, physicians, and community members through these partnership communications. But they also want an opportunity to talk back to leadership, to have their voices heard. Use traditional town halls, brown-bag lunches, ask-a-question hotlines, email or paper question boxes that can be filled out anonymously, and online social media to give your audiences the opportunity to have a dialogue with you. Let them ask the questions that are important to them and show them your confidence by welcoming the conversation. You'll build supporters, kill rumors, and affirm your position as the voice of authority.

Silence Isn't Golden

Even when you have nothing substantially new to say, staying in contact with your key audiences through frequent communication is crucial to maintaining your campaign's momentum.

Silence can be your worst enemy in a time of change. When there's silence, your staff will assume something is wrong or that important decisions are being made and not communicated because the news is bad. Rumors start to fill the vacuum. Whispered notions become "facts" that everybody knows.

Communicate so much that your audiences can't help but recite your words when they are out with friends or at church. The more your audiences know and understand your message, the more likely they are to absorb and share your vision.

It's Not Over When It's Over

Your communications plan must extend well beyond the final signing of legal documents. In fact, that signature marks the beginning of a whole new, and equally engaging, communications campaign that is less focused on details and vision and more focused on creating a new culture.

See "It's Not Over When It's Over" in Section 3 for more on culture-building through your post-close communications campaign.

Take Action: Develop a List of Materials and Communications Vehicles

For a partnership communications campaign, you should consider all the tools in your communications toolbox as you build your campaign. A few to consider:

- Holding statement
- Core messages
- Talking points for leadership, managers and directors, and board members
- FAQs: one unvarnished version to help leadership answer the tough questions and one for public and staff distribution
- Press releases
- A dedicated deal website
- Updates to your current website
- Letters (or emails) to every core audience—including patients

- Scripts for VIP phone calls your leadership will make the day before and the day of the partnership announcement
- Scripts for those who answer the phones at your hospital (Caller: "Is the hospital still open?" Switchboard: "Yes, your surgery schedule is unchanged.")

Then put all of these vehicles into a 48-hour announcement timeline that steps through your announcement day in 30-minute increments.

It's a marathon, not a sprint. Ideas for ongoing communications vehicles include:

- A stand alone-deal website
- A road show slide-show presentation for appearances at local community groups such as the Chamber of Commerce, Rotary, or other leadership groups
- A dedicated section of the employee intranet
- A section of the existing newsletter dedicated to the transition
- A weekly deal message or update from the main spokesperson

- Press conferences or media interviews at key milestone announcements
- Meetings with employee leadership
- Town hall meetings with employees held around the clock

Rule 9: Be Nimble

THE BIG IDEA

- ✦Be flexible, but don't live for every *if-then* scenario.
- ✦Shift tactics, but don't stray from your message.
- ✦Listening is key to being nimble.

Take Action: Listen, Listen, Listen

No battle plan survives contact with the enemy, says the military strategist.

You can and should plan extensively for communicating the news of your hospital partnership. You will rightly invest your time and resources into building the best approach possible. It may be the single most important communications campaign you've ever run.

But you can't plan for everything. Things happen that will surprise you. In fact, you should plan for that!

Planning for Flexibility, Not "If-Then"

You know this: People will surprise you, especially people who are stressed or threatened by change. It may be an out-of-nowhere question from the media, an off-the-wall reaction from your physicians, or an unexpected turn by regulators or from the competition. An unforeseen challenge may become a glitch that can delay the deal or change its terms.

In truth, in a significant hospital transition, it's not a question of whether there will be a twist. It's just a matter of when and from where it comes. Some hospitals attempt to plan for the unexpected through multilayered scenario planning. It's a litany of "IF this happens, THEN we'll do that." Constructing streamlined if-then plans on likely and significant challenges is wise.

However, the number of if-then plans you can create is infinite. Deliberately thinking through the ramifications of every worst-case scenario you can imagine—and you can imagine a lot—can become an overwhelming distraction.

Instead, prepare your leadership to be flexible and nimble as you move through the partnership communications process.

Remind them that a hospital partnership is not a fire-and-forget announcement. It's more like a campfire that, once started, requires constant tending.

But how do you remain true to your communications strategy while being flexible and responsive to the audiences that matter to you?

Shift Tactics, but Don't Stray From Your Message

Here is the key: Be willing to shift your tactics but not willing to stray from your message.

Here's what we mean: You may find that you need to expand your physician messaging because a rumor is spreading about a change in the nonphysician credentialing process because of the partnership. Stick to your key core message while you are correcting the rumors, but revisit your communications tactics. You may create a physician advisory council. You may have your CEO and chief medical officer (CMO) meet with your major referral sources. These steps were not part of your original campaign strategy, but the actions are an important signal that must be sent to keep the partnership moving forward.

Though these actions are new, your core message remains unchanged. In fact, these new actions become more vehicles through which you can reinforce your core message.

Reference them again and again as you pivot to address specific challenges. For example:

- This is the threat we face
- This is our bold vision for the future
- This is the solution that will get us there

Take Action: Listen, Listen, Listen

In announcing a hospital partnership, you are beginning what is sure to be a dynamic conversation in your community. You must monitor it from day one and, when you can, join it.

Do not let your leadership make the mistake of deeming the announcement a success because the first wave of media coverage was positive and the community didn't storm your hospital lobby. Don't let them slip back into the C-suite bunker.

Keep your eyes and ears open. The closer you are to your key audiences, the faster you can address questions and tackle challenges before they become problems. By listening, you can also discover unexpected opportunities and advocates who can help you succeed.

Invest your time in listening. It'll pay off.

Here are a few ways to keep your radar up:

- **Polling:** The best quantitative approach to listening is to survey your key stakeholders in a statistically valid poll. A preannouncement survey can be especially helpful in understanding the position of your key audiences and their relationship with (and level of support for) your hospital. This information can greatly inform the development of your core message and can be a powerful message, especially with elected officials.
- **Coffee:** After the first wave of announcement activity is settled and steadily moving forward over the course of the partnership transaction, sit down informally, one-on-one with handpicked influencers and ask:
  - What do you think?
  - What do you hear?
  - What's on your mind?
  - What would you do if you were me?

This is an important listening role not only for you but also for your leadership team. It's likely your CEO will be able to chat with different influencers than you or your chief nursing officer. Take advantage of your unique relationships.

Approach this deliberately. Make a list, make assignments among leadership, set deadlines, and set a time to regroup afterward to hear what has been learned.

Warning: Without this deliberate approach to listening, leadership can get caught in a reinforcing echo chamber. They hear only from people who think everything is "Great!" or (conversely and oddly) they only hear from people who believe the hospital is sliding into unmitigated chaos. Either way, it's skewed and unhelpful information.

- **Go back to your advocates:** We talk in Rule 7 about building a grassroots team for the partnership transaction. If you've built it correctly, you will have a living focus group with representatives from a cross-section of your organization and community. This group may have helped you build a core message and become advocates (and translators) of the partnership. Engage them now as a living focus group. Ask them:

- Is it working?
- What are we doing right?
- What needs to change?
- What did we miss?

Rule 10: Don't Dance to Someone Else's Music

THE BIG IDEA

✦ Don't allow the criticism or challenges of others to direct what you are going to say, or when and how you say it.

Take Action: Respond Responsibly

Your board chair wakes up in the morning and, over a cup of coffee, reads a nasty letter to the editor in the newspaper about your hospital and its partnership plans.

The letter is angry, uninformed, and heavily biased. It hinges on a personal experience that clouds all other considerations. Acerbic and equally subjective online reader comments pile on, adding fuel to the fire.

The board chair, wounded and incensed, calls you.

"I want a full-page ad in response to this jerk," she says. "I want to send a letter to everyone in the community. I want you to call the editor of the paper and demand a front-page story that fixes this and have them delete those online comments while you're at it. And get something out to our physicians, too."

With this, the author of that letter to the editor has been put in charge of your communications strategy. You've moved from offense to defense.

The Risk of Losing the Lead

It's an old saying: "Don't dance to somebody else's music." You don't allow the criticism or challenges of others to direct your strategy and change what you are going to say and when and how you say it.

Why?

When you respond to these attacks—usually designed by your opponent to hurt your deal and nothing more—it's easy to be defensive. Your emotion and hard work are invested in the partnership.

But when you make the attack worthy of your time, you delight the troublemaker and cause your supporters to question your response: "Why are they responding to that nut? Are they seriously worried about that?" Your credibility dives and the attacker's credibility rises.

What's worse is that the majority of people may have not even heard the criticism until you elevated it with a response. It's like the old media training rule: Never repeat the negative. It only gives the opposition legs.

See the snowball effect? You're off-message and distracted from the core threat, vision, and solution message that you must communicate.

This rule is not just for media issues. It's just as important for testy physician interactions, labor matters, and potential challenges. Attacks and distractions come from all corners.

A good question to ask when attacked and determining whether to respond is this: Will the story die by itself once printed, especially if you don't feed it with a response? If yes, then don't respond.

If you must respond

If your answer to the previous question is no, then you have to *consider* a response.

Remember, most sparks go out by themselves. A few ignite forest fires. You cannot treat all attacks the same. You and your leadership team must be able to discern the difference. Here are a few rules of thumb to help you make your decision:

- **Separate the smoke from the fire.** This is challenge No. 1. Cut through the bad blood, tangled relationships, and competitive personalities to the factual issues.

- **Be tightly focused in your response.** If the attack comes from 10 physicians, address it with those 10 physicians instead of sending memos to the entire medical staff.

- **Stay on message.** Bridge any response back to your core message for the campaign. Do not stray and do not linger on the criticism. Why give it that power over your message?

- **Be brief.** No doubt the issue that led to the criticism is complicated and thorny. Underneath a specific charge is probably mistrust, anger, or fear. These emotions will not be repaired with words only. Acknowledge the issue, defuse it with your response quickly, and move on to your core, forward-looking message. If some want to dive into the details, don't let them: You have other serious business to attend to.

- **Be authoritative in tone.** An angry response to an angry attack is a missed opportunity to demonstrate the strength of your position. Your authoritative tone should almost be parental: This is not a condescending tenor, but one that can acknowledge the issue while expressing confidence in the organization and its future, even despite the attack. It's unruffled, caring, and rock-solid.

- **Be quick.** If you must respond, do so with speed and finality. Do not let the matter grow and spread.

- **Be measured.** Make the response fit the attack. Does a letter to the editor deserve a full-page newspaper ad as a response? Are you protesting too much?

- **Everyone is watching.** When you are in a leadership position, every action or inaction is a message. Every action or inaction can be perceived as a strategic choice. Make sure your actions—not just your words—send the message you intend.

Vacuums Breed Attacks

If you don't have anything to say, your opponents will be sure to take advantage.

Further, silence implies guilt or hiding. So whether or not you have been attacked, people will notice if you fall silent in such an emotional time as a transaction. They'll start to wonder why you aren't sharing updates. Is the deal falling apart? Are they hatching new plans that threaten jobs?

You are most vulnerable when you are not consistently and assertively communicating with the audiences that matter to you throughout the partnership process.

It's more effective to constantly communicate that nothing new is taking place than to refute rumors and respond to baseless attacks.

Take Action: Don't Abandon "Everyday" Campaigns

Many hospitals are armored against significant critical sniping by the strength of their reputation and their relationships. If you have that strength, use it to stay above the fray. You have other things on your mind. Act like it.

Before the announcement takes place, solidify the other areas of your work that add credibility to your case. For example:

- **Testimonial campaigns.** It's one thing to attack a C-suite member who wears a suit to work every day. It's another to come up against the community physician in a white coat who has served the community for three decades, or a nurse who works on the OB wing, or a patient who owes his or her life to your care. If you're running a testimonial campaign, reup your contracts, add new stories, or increase your buys. If not, consider a small and targeted campaign. It's not time to spin up something grand and shiny, but a handful of strategically placed stories gives third-party credibility to your hospital.

- **Quality.** Hospitals are always and increasingly under the microscope when it comes to quality—more so when the inner workings of your hospital are the subject of ongoing media stories. In case your community starts to wonder if the transaction is happening because quality is suffering, make sure that what you do best is highlighted in the community. One tactic is to create a "State of the Hospital" road show that includes details of the deal (once announced) and that highlights how excellent your quality is today. Compare it to that of your competitors. If you're achieving the same or better outcomes, tell your community. Bonus points if you are doing it at a lower cost.

- **Contributions and sponsorships.** As long as you plan to maintain your sponsorships of community events and groups, tout what you're doing in advance of the transaction announcement. It will convey the message that the impending partnership only makes your ties to the community all the stronger. Further, in the event any of these sponsors are asked for comment about the relationship, their endorsement of your support to date and anticipated backing even after the partnership takes place will only build the groundswell of support.

Section 3

OF PARTICULAR NOTE ...

The Power of Digital Media

When it comes to digital media—websites, social sites, newspaper forums—the question is not *if* you should participate. It's really *when.*

By the time this book publishes, there will be a shiny new tool on the Web. So instead of looking at each tool that may be out of date, say, tomorrow, we'll take a look at some key issues and principles of using the Web to your advantage in a partnership campaign.

And what an advantage it can be.

Wherever your hospital stands on digital media today, here are a couple of thoughts:

- Your partnership campaign is a great opportunity to use these tools to engage a variety of audiences in new ways.
- If you are behind, you're not alone.
- A few simple and familiar yet unique steps can have a powerful impact.

Taking the most advantage of the opportunity means looking at your campaign as something unique—not just an event or an announcement, but a campaign. The same dedication you give to the entire communications campaign offline needs to be applied online.

The key is this: Don't try to do every digital idea all at once. If you are already running a robust digital media campaign, congratulations and keep going with your daily work. If you aren't doing anything, then remember that even small steps can make an impact.

> Don't worry! In this chapter, we will answer the burning question of what to do with negative comments online. As a first step, reread Rule 4: Think Like the Opposition and Rule 10: Don't Dance to Someone Else's Music, which offer advice on how to manage naysayers, opposition, and challenges in general. These same principles can be applied to the online world. Remember, deciding whether to answer a comment is about more than just taking an "answer this, don't answer that" approach.

Simple Yet Unique: Why a Deal Website Matters

Throughout this book, we talk about the idea of building a deal website. This is a site completely and solely dedicated to your deal. It's not a page on your hospital site. It stands alone. Why?

Creating a Web presence like this is a signal. It says to your community, "This is important. We know you will be seeking information at all hours of the day. Here it is on a silver platter."

That "silver platter" statement may cause you to fret about building the Taj Mahal of healthcare websites. Maybe you're thinking the deal website must have videos, moving features, and interactivity that requires a response to everything. If you can do that (and afford it), great. But it's not necessary for a deal site to be valuable to you.

Even the simplest sites—for example, six total pages of material you are already writing for other communication vehicles—become high-traffic destinations for media, community members, elected officials, staff members, and patients.

This happens because, when faced with such an emotional change as a partnership, people find great comfort in seeing an answer or piece of information on a trusted source online.

So when you think about a deal website, think about simple graphics, limited interactivity, and a chance to just get your message out to the community the way you want.

> You will likely want to consider an outside resource to create a site that is completely separate from your existing site. The first reason is that this is a signal to your core audiences that what's about to happen is new, important, and critical to get right. In addition, you will likely need to get a site like this up very quickly. Often, outside vendors are able to meet a quick turnaround better than internal departments.

Elements of a deal website

Think of your website as a practical microcosm of your M&A communications campaign. As the hub of all external communication, certainly this site is also a key resource for your internal audiences. This makes it one of the strongest tools in your toolbox.

Although it doesn't have to be fancy, your stand-alone site must be as nimble as possible. Your campaign team should adopt the mentality that this site must be able to change on a dime, provide real-time updates, and be easily customized to the audiences you want to reach.

Choose a vendor (or have your internal IT team choose a platform) that can give you the ability to edit content on your own through a content management system. These are backend portals to your site that let you easily access each page and edit the content in a program that works like your word processor. When you need to get a message out, or an important piece of information has changed, you don't want to wait in a Web firm's queue to get a simple yet important edit made.

Broadly speaking, these are the critical elements you should include on your site:

- **A warm, personal message:** This should feel like the opposite of corporatese. A letter written jointly from both organizations' leaders is a powerful communication tool that can become the home page of your site. It should hit all of the highlights of your core message but through the human lens of two people who care deeply about each organization.
- **A graphic identity:** The deal website is a prime place to use your partnership campaign graphics in a prominent way. While you should still include a link back to each hospital's site, as well as fact sheets on both organizations, the deal site can stand alone in design and look because it is a unique campaign. Logos, colors, etc., should be consistent to present a cohesive look and feel.

- **Simple navigation:** There's no need to overwhelm or be extra creative with how you name the pages on this site. The following site map should do the trick, so that people can easily get the information they need:
  - Home page
  - About the vision
  - Why change?
  - For patients
  - For employees
  - FAQs
  - Ask a question
  - What's next?
  - In the news

> A special note on the In the News section: You will find that news media will use this site all the time. They also will check the FAQs and return to this page frequently for updates. They will drive their readers to the site, and it will be a key resource to them. Keep that in mind, and make it helpful. Also be mindful that anything and everything on this site should be appropriate to appear in the newspaper.

- **Callout boxes:** You don't need to have all eight sections in tabs across the top of the home page. Some of the most important pieces can be included in graphic boxes on the home page, called out with special attention. Your "For employees" section is one that should stand out. You want your employees to remember that this site is not just an external-facing tool. It should also be easy for them to access, since many will have to do so at home.

  You can also use a callout box to highlight information such as: the benefits of your partnership, so many millions of dollars invested, new service lines created, all jobs preserved. Testimonials from community leaders that include a simple quote of endorsement are also powerful to call out in this manner.

- **FAQs and soliciting questions:** Your FAQ section should be based on your core message and reiterate your threat, vision, and solution in a question-and-answer format. Certainly provide a little more detail than you do in your messaging, but don't make it so full of additional details that it feels like a completely new source of information. It's also a good place to add information that isn't necessarily important enough to make the press release but that you know will be on the minds of your audiences.

You should also set up a section where individuals can anonymously ask a question that is emailed to your team. This enables your audiences to express their thoughts and ask questions that are on their mind. On most user-managed website platforms with a content management system, this is an easy tool to create. It's likely already a template that your designer can customize.

The key to managing this is to manage expectations on the front end by making a statement that you will answer the most often-asked questions. This relieves you of the need to email every single individual with a response or post information that you are not ready to post. If you have the resources, assign one team member to gather the questions each week. If that person is you, monitor the questions each day but set aside a time each week to really determine which ones need an answer publicly.

> How long does this site last? Surely through the deal announcement and close. At that time, you may start to transition the graphics and language into content that fits the new entity. Eventually the site goes away or morphs into the new entity's site. Just like you know when it's time to end any other campaign, you will know when it's time to turn off the site.

The Next Step: Social Media

Whether or not you choose to engage in social media on this deal, someone else will. It's that classic caveat: When you don't tell your story, there is someone waiting in the wings with their own script.

> This guide focuses on hospital partnership communications. It's not an expert guide to managing your social media campaign, so we'll keep our comments on social media short. There are plenty of resources specific to healthcare in that realm—all it takes to unearth them is a Web search. We recommend resources such as the Mayo Clinic Center for Social Media.

Some hospitals have no social media presence; others tweet around the clock. Regardless of where you are today, smart hospitals will:

- Reserve

- Listen
- Engage

Reserve

Both for your hospital name and for the campaign theme, reserve your names (combined or alone), handles, URLs, and other user names and accounts on all platforms—even if you don't plan to use them just yet. You can also consider creating accounts on your local newspaper forums with those same names so that you can engage in conversation there.

If you don't reserve these user names and accounts, someone else—your opposition, perhaps—may choose to do it "for you." This ties your hands in the event you see the need to do this down the road.

It could also be a source of confusion. Whether or not you promote any Web presence, your audiences will likely just assume that you are there and go searching for you. If it's a blank page, or, worse yet, your opposition has taken the space for you to share their opinion on the partnership, your audiences will be filled with anything but the story you want to tell.

URLs are inexpensive in most cases—we're talking $10 a year. The return on investment is nearly priceless. The cost is time and attention.

Listen

Here's the key benefit of social media: It's an intelligence-gathering machine. You may not comment or participate in a visible way. But you should watch, search, and "listen" to what others are saying on all platforms. It sounds exhausting, but think of it as a free focus group. Even if you have to spend some time on it out of the office because sites are blocked, it's worth the investment.

There are tools to make this listening easier. Do a search for "social media management" and review the organic and advertisement results. There will be several free and paid options.

Engage

If you do choose to engage on social media, one key priority is this: Monitor local newspaper forums, especially if you live in a smaller community.

Even if your audiences are not on Facebook, they likely look at the websites of their favorite local paper. Many stories include a forum at the end of the story. Like chat rooms of Internet generations past, these forums allow anyone to say anything they want (as long as it's not crass, according to the newspaper's standards).

When you monitor coverage on newspaper websites, pay attention to the comments. If they are positive, excellent. You may consider adding a few comments of your own that reiterate a core message or thank the reader. You can include your stand-alone website URL, too.

If they are negative, you have to consider the best way to respond. Reread Rule 4: Think Like the Opposition and Rule 10: Don't Dance to Someone Else's Music. Each has good tips for determining when to give weight to a negative comment and when to let it sit without a response.

Correcting misinformation is likely a safe and necessary route to take. Getting into a public dialogue on the merits of your deal with someone who left a comment on the newspaper website may be less of a good idea. Sometimes a comment can be as simple as, "I'm sorry you feel that way. Our commitment is to keep you informed so that you know what's going on, and you can do that on our website at www.XXXXXX.com." Bottom line: Don't argue in public.

It's worth noting, too, what you are probably thinking: In some cases, the people who take the time to comment on news stories are the same small group of individuals, over and over. In many cases, that's true, and that should factor in to how you respond. But when determining your next steps, consider the fact that there are exponentially more people who read those comments, even if just for entertainment value. So there is an opportunity for you to educate others.

Facebook, YouTube, Twitter, Instagram—each social media platform also presents the opportunity for engagement. And by the time this book publishes, there will be something new and something that's hot today will have faded into the background. So explore social media platforms, use them as tools to listen, and study how your community uses each. If people are using them to comment on your deal, your case for engaging them just went up. If your community is slow to use these tools, then you may be able to move a little more slowly on it.

If you do choose to engage, get creative and remember that it does not need to be a resource drain. Simplicity, organic content that does not feel "produced," candidness, dialogue, visual presentation of your ideas, and timeliness rule the day with social media.

The point here is this: Though carrying some risk, social media offers an amazing window into how your audiences respond to your core message. It's like a real-time focus group. It's always better to know what others think about you—and have the opportunity to respond when warranted—than to stick your head in the sand.

Hurdling the Barriers of Social Media

Given the millions of monthly users, shockingly few hospitals and healthcare systems take advantage of the power of social media.

Why do we shy away from it? We fear the comments. We have to comply with patient confidentiality issues and HIPAA. It's not as big in our community as others. We have to be careful of how labor unions will react. We don't have time.

Each of these reasons is important, but they can all be worked through. Every case is different.

Managing comments

A key question we hear is whether to turn on the comments feature on the site. Leave comments on because, in a fast-paced campaign such as the one you face with a partnership, they can be a true rumor killer.

Thinking back on two key principles—the seven times rule and speaking even when there is no news—Facebook can be a great rumor killer. Yes, this is a point worth repeating because it's a little surprising. It's a chance to reiterate over and over your core message, the latest update, the next step, or simply a reassurance that all is going well.

You may be thinking that those comments just start rumors. This is where you have to do some weighing of pros and cons. On the pro side of comments, you can interact with supportive audiences and correct misinformation if it appears. On the con side, misinformation and contrary opinions will be posted, challenging your message.

Time

Another universal issue is this: resources. When it comes down to it, the lack of resources can be your greatest challenge. After all, if you are in a partnership campaign, you likely have constraints on budgets as well as a lot to do.

In your partnership phase, your entire team (and we realize that could just be you) will be swamped with work. Not only do you have your daily campaigns to run, but you also have the critical, difficult core message to send about the future of the hospital.

How do you know what is being said about you online? Here are four tools:

- **Google Search:** A quick Google search of your facility name and the M&A campaign you are going through can give you a snapshot of what's out there already.
- **Twitter hashtag search:** Search Twitter for hashtags involving your facility name.
- **LinkedIn blogs:** Keep an eye on LinkedIn blogs for discussions about your M&A deal. Also, this can be a good forum to find others talking about healthcare M&As; they could be possible supporters.
- **News search:** As always, you will want to stay aware of the news, and the news your opposition and supporters are sharing. Google News and Google Alerts are great tools that pull most results, usually in real time.

One way to handle this is to carve out the time even just to monitor. If you have a team, that means assigning the task to one person. If it's just you in communications, carve out 15 minutes every morning to take a look. You may even consider asking one of your advocates who is already personally connected on multiple social media platforms to be the point person. Again, find a good social media management aggregator. This can save you a world of time.

Engaging employees

This is an age-old debate, if issues of social media can be "age-old."

Healthcare organizations have traditionally blocked outside, popular websites—any page that has nothing to do with hospital business as well as simple social media sites—out of a concern for productivity and control over Internet access. However, smartphones and tablets changed the game; there's no blocking them.

So in the midst of your partnership, consider at least allowing access to your stand-alone site and the local newspaper. These are your two online priorities in your partnership campaign. You will likely have to work with IT on this one.

> Healthcare organizations also block these sites due to patient privacy issues or managing relations with organized labor. Neither should be an impediment to allowing access to these sites, though in reality that often is the case. It may be a hurdle you can't overcome, too, because of IT issues. In these cases, it's worth spending the time at home monitoring online media—because your supporters and your opposition are doing just that.

Here's why access to these sites can be helpful:

- **Stand-alone site:** You want your employees to get the same information as the newspaper and the regulatory authorities, so keep the information that external as well as internal audiences need on the deal site. Doing so gives everyone the whole picture. You can also allow employees to feel more anonymous in asking a question through your FAQ page on that site, rather than on the hospital intranet, where they likely have an account.
- **Newspaper sites:** There will come a day in your campaign where you need to activate your employees to counter negative messages in the newspaper story comments section. Their comments can't wait until after their shift, because you need to counter the commentary now and you can't expect them to prioritize that over their home life. By allowing access to these sites at work, you let them participate in advocating for your partnership.

If you do have the ability to allow access to social media sites, then use that permission to your advantage. Be sure you offer staff commentary to share on the partnership if they choose. Help them with their messaging if they want assistance. You would have helped them write a letter to the editor for the paper, so why not a tweet for Twitter?

If you don't already have one, it's time to create a social media policy that applies hospitalwide. There are examples of such policies all over the Internet, but you should spell out everything that you want to happen. Then, publicize the policy so your employees are never caught off guard, and turn your harnessing into an issue of free speech.

So Do I Turn On or Up the Social Media Now?

This is a great question that doesn't have an across-the-board answer.

You need to reserve your pages, user names, and URLs in social media. If you're already in that world, you may be considering how much to crank up the volume.

Your next step really is to read your staff and your community and ask:

- Are there audiences we have never reached out there?
- Is this big enough news that you might gain patients or referrals simply by introducing yourself to those new audiences through this event?

- How active is your local community in social media?

Whatever you do, take it step by step. Start slow if you need to. But know that the online world is an excellent place to share your story, and an excellent way for it to be shared for you in your stead.

Troubleshooting: What to Do When ...

Now that you have read the rules, you may be left with two thoughts:

1. "Wow. That was immensely helpful."
2. "Yes, but they still didn't tell me what to do when [insert your unique situation here]."

Now comes the tough part: troubleshooting.

Certainly, every partnership case is different and every situation unique. There are particular issues that must be dealt with and tailored, but the rules still apply.

So with the rules as a foundation, this section discusses some of those more sticky and unique situations and offers pointers for what to pay attention to in each scenario. Then, adapt the action items paired with each of the 10 rules to your situation.

> Important note: In the section that follows, we offer the lightest touches on what can be tremendously difficult issues. However, these recommendations—particularly when used in conjunction with the 10 rules—can get you moving in the right direction.

Faith-Based to Secular Conversion

When a 100-plus-year-old, faith-based, not-for-profit community hospital is purchased by an investor-owned organization, there is an inevitable challenge to face: the loss of religious identity. The emotions surrounding the sale of a hospital are highly sensitive. Compound this with the emotions surrounding a strongly held religious faith, and you've got a powder keg to defuse.

The issues stemming from a faith-based conversion can range from practical (and traditional) decision-making practices to charity care policies and foundational culture matters.

A few examples:

- Can nurses still pray on their units and with patients once the sale is complete?
- Will your hospital still accommodate (and fund) a chaplaincy program?

- What about the ethical and religious directives (ERD)? ERDs are those related to women's reproductive health and end-of-life issues followed by Catholic and other religious hospitals. After your new partnership is complete, do the ERDs vanish?

Being acutely aware of these and other issues will help you avoid easily triggered land mines in a faith-based conversion. Know the answers to the questions in the previous list as soon as possible. If they are not being discussed, ask them.

Early on, identify the local religious leader(s) who will be influential to the success of the new partnership. If working with Catholic sponsors, that may be the bishop for the region. It may be a sister who leads a local order. More broadly, it may be the head of a denomination. That person may not be directly involved in official decision-making, but his or her opinion and endorsement matter. Even more importantly, his or her disapproval—even if only on the grounds of being uninvolved in the transition—may impact the deal and the momentum you hope to carry once the transaction closes.

Educate yourself on the unique approval process in a faith-based transaction. You may be thousands of miles away, but—for example—the Catholic church in Rome has a say in finalizing any Catholic hospital conversion. A separate application for approval will go to an office in Rome, which will add time (and possibly its own politics) to the process. Be aware of similar processes for other faith traditions.

Recognize the emotion of removing religious symbols from the hospital. When a religious hospital converts to a nonreligious entity, it can go through a "decommissioning." This can include removing treasured religious symbols from the facility. The removal of the artifacts and the loss this represents can be an emotionally charged event. Work with the sponsors of the hospital to create a plan that respects the hospital's religious tradition and recognizes the transition.

In some cases, hospital and local religious authorities stage a ceremony honoring its faith heritage. Others create a designated public area of the hospital where these religious symbols and the hospital's history are honored in old photographs and other memorabilia.

Recognize the emotional connection patients make with religion-based care. Many find comfort in receiving their care at a hospital rooted in religious history and a faith-based mission. Nonreligious ownership will have an impact even on patients and staff who do not explicitly follow one particular faith.

In some cases, religious leaders are appointed to the board of the new partnership to help guide it going forward. In other cases, the new owners share their own faith traditions with staff and others to signal the continued value leaders place on the spiritual side of care delivery.

Not-for-Profit to Investor-Owned Conversion

In most communities, the conversion of a hospital from a not-for-profit to an investor-owned enterprise no longer stirs the heated debate that it did decades ago. Instead, you're much more likely today to see not-for-profit and investor-owned hospital organizations working in partnership.

Renowned not-for-profit health systems such as Duke University Medical Center and The Cleveland Clinic have formed strong affiliations with investor-owned hospital companies. In these and other partnerships, not-for-profits and investor-owned organizations are working together to strengthen hospitals, invest in communities, and serve patients.

In fact, the issues facing investor-owned hospital systems during a partnership are the same as those faced by not-for-profit health systems during a partnership discussion: Local control and governance, cultural compatibility, charity care support, and commitment to local investment are leading hot buttons for both.

Still, the "conversion" of a not-for-profit for an investor-owned organization can represent a change that can sometimes raise questions and ignite unhelpful rumors.

To help you be prepared, let's start by answering this basic question: What's the difference? How are not-for-profit and for-profit (investor-owned) hospitals different from one another?

- **Taxes:** First, a (very) broad definition: "Not-for-profit" and "for-profit" are tax-related designations. A not-for-profit hospital does not pay certain taxes, including those on property used for care, income, and sales. However, it usually does pay payroll and other federal employee taxes. A for-profit hospital pays property, sales, and income taxes as well as payroll taxes. Not-for-profits sometimes make payments in lieu of taxes to help offset the costs of providing important community services such as police and fire coverage.

- **Capital:** Not-for-profit and investor-owned hospitals are also differentiated by where they get capital to invest in their facilities for infrastructure improvements, new equipment, staff, and the like. Not-for-profit hospitals usually go to the bond market for capital. Investor-owned hospitals go to the public stock market, the bond market, or investment groups for capital.

- **Analysts:** One other note related to hospital capital: Both types of organizations have outsiders judging the hospital's financial performance. Not-for-profits are "rated" by credit rating agencies, such as Moody's Investor Services and Standard & Poor's, to help investors monitor their portfolios and make buying and selling decisions. Publicly traded, investor-owned hospital stocks are watched by analysts and valued daily in stock exchanges.
- **Ownership:** Who "owns" the hospital after the sale can be an important question, and can reflect a community's concerns about having a "voice" in the care provided at its hospital in the future. The answer can be complicated, and is not always consistent from hospital to hospital, and community to community. Here's an overview:

Independent, not-for-profit hospitals are, in a sense, owned by the communities they serve. The boards are usually comprised of local leaders and physicians. Excess revenues—profits—are fully reinvested into the community's care after debt payments, payroll, and other expenses. Hospitals that join a regional or national not-for-profit health system, however, may or may not have a local board with a say in the direction of the facility, and may or may not share their profits with the system. (In fact, if your local hospital is in financial trouble, the money flows into your hospital, not out of it!)

Investor-owned hospitals are, as you might guess by the name, owned by investors, who can be private individuals or stockholders. Investors traditionally benefit as the value of the company's hospitals increase over time, through effective operations and local investments, and as the company overall grows by adding more hospitals.

Adding to this complexity is the trend for hospitals to pursue joint venture partnerships where ownership is shared by two or more organizations, including the "seller." These partnerships call for strong and trusting relationships by every party. Communications is key to success.

Familiarize yourselves with these terms and issues as you move through a partnership. Be prepared for some myth-busting.

That's where the fundamental structural differences end. The driving forces of both organizations, however, are precisely the same:

- No matter your tax status, every hospital has to take in more dollars than it spends in order to be financially healthy and to reinvest in the care it provides.
- Every hospital must offer quality care, provide current medical equipment and facilities, and support a trained staff to attract (and keep) patients and serve the needs of physicians, payers, and others.

Now, consider some specific questions you may hear related to the structure of a not-for-profit to investor-owned conversion.

What happens to the proceeds of the sale?

When there are funds left over from a sale, they are often referred to as the proceeds. These proceeds exist once the hospital's debt and any other obligations (e.g., a pension fund) have been paid.

The answer as to what happens to those dollars depends on the ownership structure of the selling organization and the terms of the transaction. Here are a few scenarios:

- The sale of a stand-alone, not-for-profit community hospital to an investor-owned company may lead to the creation of a community foundation. The creation of the foundation—including its board and mission—may be directed by your state attorney general's office and the proceeds from the sale will fund it.
- When two not-for-profits merge, it is rare that there are proceeds. Instead, the common practice is for all assets from both organizations to combine for the good of the new system.
- From the sale of a hospital owned by a religious organization, the remaining proceeds will likely return to that order or denomination.
- From the sale of a government-owned hospital, the money left over may return to the city or county's coffers, which may deposit the money into the government's general operating fund or create a new organization for meeting the charitable healthcare needs of the community.

Will charity care continue at its current level?

This is really a question of community commitment and may be an indicator of how much the community-based culture is or is not going to change under the new ownership. In most cases, a commitment to either a specific level of charity care or a guarantee to continue the hospital's existing charitable mission and charity care policy is written into the deal documents. Expect the question and know the answer.

How much money in local taxes will the new hospital owner pay?

An investor-owned hospital pays taxes that benefit local government. This question is an opportunity to highlight the added contribution as a distinct benefit of investor-owned partnerships.

In many cases, the fire department, police force, schools, parks, and other community assets will benefit on an annual basis from an investor-owned partner paying state and local property and sales taxes.

One note of caution: In some cases, new hospital owners may seek appropriate tax incentives when entering a new community and investing in a hospital. Be sure you understand the local government strategic thinking before you answer the tax question.

Name Change

A name change in a merger or acquisition does not always occur, but it is a consideration that always accompanies a change of ownership. When you need to change the name of your hospital or health system, consider the following:

- **Make it short.** Whatever you name the new hospital, people will shorten it to a two-syllable identifier. St. Bartholomew's Medical Center will be St. Bart's. Northern Peninsula Health System will be North Penn. Expect the community editing and craft your new name so it's what you want to hear when people speak and write in shorthand.
- **The old name will stick.** For years. Out of habit and loyalty, your community and staff are likely to use the old name until the new one—your new brand—reflects both a place where people want to serve and an experience people want to have. Building and promoting the story of the benefits of your new partnership is critical so that the brand change is not

so stark and, instead, is allowed to become a natural evolution of the organization.

- **People will think the name is odd.** Well, yes: It's new and it's different and people don't like change. If it's a made-up name, if it's a long name because you have joined a system, or if it's a combined name to reflect the joint nature of the partnership, no doubt your constituents will poke holes in it. That's okay. Give it time. It's rare that the challenge you'll truly face is the new name; it's what the new name represents. Focus on promoting the new path for your organization and less on the name. If the former is accepted, the latter will come.
- **Who names the hospital?** In some cases, the new name will be prescribed, perhaps by a system nomenclature or by the community the hospital serves. But if you have the leeway, you may consider involving your internal audiences and even your community in the naming process. Have contests, focus groups, and other publicly announced methods of soliciting ideas for a new hospital name. The process is another way to engage the community in the hospital and its future. If you choose this route, deliberately letting the community know that the name came from their neighbors and celebrating that fact is important.

Antitrust Concerns

A brief search online will show the Federal Trade Commission's (FTC) increased scrutiny of hospital partnerships, especially when service areas of the partnering health system overlap or the government suspects the partnership may be anticompetitive. Partnerships supported by both parties have been delayed, lingered in the courts for months and years, and sometimes finally blocked by FTC action.

If your potential partnership is a candidate for FTC review, this should affect all of your partnership communications activity from your first announcement to the close of the transaction.

Take this seriously. From day one.

Work closely with your legal counsel

If FTC review is even a slight possibility, chances are your general counsel or your board has also engaged special antitrust counsel to study the marketplace and assist in the transaction. Engage with them throughout the deal.

Watch your outside language

If your partnership transaction is being examined by the FTC, the regulators will watch closely for signals of the intention driving the deal.

One way they can understand your intent is to study how you describe the goals of the transaction. Are you going to "dominate" the market by coming together? Will you "own" the town? Will this make you "competitive?" Do you want "scale" and "market power?" Will the partnership finally allow you to "push back" against bullying insurance companies? Will you "get control" over your unruly independent physicians? Will you be able to "kill" the competition?

These are not the words and phrases you want to use in either official communications or in off-the-cuff remarks by your CEO at the Rotary meeting. It's easy to imagine how these signals can attract FTC attention.

Instead, focus on how the partnership will improve the quality of care that your organizations can deliver today, how the patient experience will be enhanced, the services that will be offered by combining your resources, and the jobs that will be saved or brought into the community. It's a healthcare message, not a business dominance message.

Watch your inside language

The internal emails are the stumbling blocks. It's the other place regulators may look to understand the intent driving the hospital partnership.

It's not merely the copy on your website, the official press release, or the public comments that are studied by government reviewers. Included, too, are the everyday internal email exchanges between you and your leaders related to the deal—the off-hand comment, or the victory yelp, or the should-have-been-funny-but-wasn't cutting remark that can trip you up.

In this environment, you should communicate—internally and externally, formally and informally—as if every written email, document, and captured-on-tape comment will be seen and weighed by the FTC or the court.

Respect the regulator

Every hospital transaction requires some level of government review. Until that review is completed, there is no deal. In your public and private messages, be sure to clearly acknowledge the important and appropriate role of regulators in the transaction process. For a simple example, in your announcement press release, avoid saying, "The transaction will be completed March 1." Say, instead, "We hope the transaction will be complete this spring pending review and approval by appropriate government agencies."

Respect the community

Government processes are political processes. Government is us, after all. Everyone is influenced by the politics and perceived support (or perceived lack of support) for the proposed partnership.

Your mission is to create a community environment in which it is politically safe and appropriate for regulators to approve the partnership that will take your hospital forward. Creating this environment is the underlying theme throughout this guide. Did we mention that you should work with your legal counsel? It's worth saying twice.

A mission of the FTC is to protect payers and patients from falling victim to healthcare monopolies. In its review of a hospital partnership, the FTC directly contacts community leaders, independent physicians, and business executives to gain their perspective on the hospital deal. It's a telephone survey, in a sense, asking how well you've delivered your message to the community. Your job is to win that vote.

Winning the Public Referendum

The political campaign approach has been used as a metaphor in this guide. Sometimes publicly owned hospitals have to run a true political campaign to win a referendum for approval of the partnership.

How do you win at the polls? In addition to following the 10 rules, consider these classic campaign tips:

- **Political messaging:** In addition to your partnership core messages (threat, vision, solution), you must consider the political environment in which voters make decisions. Ponder these questions as you develop your message and campaign strategy:
  - Who is likely to vote? Not every citizen, or even every registered voter will vote. Who actually goes to the polls in your market? How many of them are your employees, spouses, vendors, volunteers, friends, etc.?
  - Is your partnership part of a regularly scheduled ballot during a hotly contested election cycle or a stand-alone issue vote? The former will help drive voter turnout. The latter will likely have much fewer participants.

- What will drive your voters to approve your deal? It may not be one of your core healthcare-related messages. The key message may be about reducing taxes, protecting jobs, preserving local control of healthcare, getting a multimillion-dollar foundation, or getting the liability of owning a hospital off the city's balance sheet. Create, test, and use the message that drives your vote.

- **Government:** It's political parlance for a "get out the vote" style campaign. In this case, it's not enough for your key audiences to appreciate and support your hospital partnership; they have to *do* something about it. There's action they have to take. They have to vote (and vote in your favor). It's government that leads to the campaign paraphernalia you know and love: yard signs, bumper stickers, flyers, TV and radio ads, email blasts, etc. To win a vote, you have to do ***more*** than win the hearts and minds of your community. You have to drive action.

- **Advocates or formal grassroots groups:** We discussed this in Rule 7: An Army of Advocates; advocates, and particularly grassroots groups, must be built up and sent out. Like all of us, grassroots campaign teams are energized when they have a specific goal to win, and there are few things more specific than winning an election. Organize your team and let them go to work for you. This grassroots support is fundamental to winning.

Facility Repurposing

Hospitals sometimes close and are reborn as something new.

In today's evolving environment where financial incentives are moving toward keeping patients out of acute care settings, the need for some hospitals to continue as purely hospitals is going away.

Sometimes a partnership allows a fading hospital to be transformed or repurposed into a multipurpose healthcare site that can include ambulatory surgery centers, stand-alone emergency departments, physician offices, rehabilitation centers, and more.

This transformation may be exactly the right development for healthcare delivery in the community. But it can be a difficult change for nearby residents and staff nonetheless. Keep the following in mind:

- **Be clear.** In your communications, be crystal clear about the change to the facility, why it's needed, how patient care will be protected (or enhanced), and the impact on local jobs. No qualified language about "maybe" or "possibly" or "we're exploring ..." Rip off the bandage. Be up front. Be personal.

- **Explain why.** Chances are one reason behind the change is that the patient volumes no longer support the high cost of staffing, equipping, and maintaining an acute care facility or providing safe and quality care 24 hours a day. Say that. Show the numbers. It won't be pretty, but it's not supposed to be.
- **Use a map.** Show everyone where they will need to go for emergency care. An emergency department (ED) close to home is important to everyone. If you are closing this ED, make it clear how to get to the next one and how long it takes. (It's also another opportunity to differentiate between true emergency care and urgent care.)
- **Be clear about job loss.** If there is a loss of jobs—if the jobs cannot be absorbed into the new partnership—tell staff the bad news at the earliest possible time and be as specific as possible about who and how many will be terminated and when it will occur. You will also need to consider the implications of the U.S. Department of

Labor's Worker Adjustment and Retraining Notification (WARN) Act in your communication vehicles and timeline. The WARN Act requires most employers with more than 100 employees to give 60 calendar days notice of closings or mass layoffs. If you can, conduct job fairs with other healthcare organizations.

- **Change patient and physician habits.** With this change, you are introducing to nearby physicians, their office managers, and their patients a new way of thinking and working. Execute a multimonth campaign to educate these groups on where to get care, how to connect to your new system, and where to find you. Sweep a market with door hangers, launch microsites, engage with local churches and social service agencies, conduct phone trees, and more to canvas a community. Others have found success in having lunch-and-learns with area primary care physicians and office managers.

What's more, you'll want to equip your physicians, phone operators, receptionists, front-desk volunteers, and other first-point-of-contact individuals with talking points so they are ready to be helpful.

It's Not Over When It's Over

In a hospital partnership, the day the transaction is completed is only the beginning.

Why?

Because now it's time to move from theory to action, from dream to reality.

Staff members, nurses, physicians, patients, and community members will want to know, "Okay, now what?" Their questions will become more pointed, and they will expect you to know the answers—after all, you're on the same team now, right?

It is easy to imagine their concerns. Here are some examples:

- **From staff:** What will it be like to work with "them"? How will my job change? What are the new expectations? How will it feel? How long will I give it to work before deciding to look elsewhere? Will we lose our identity? Will we be submerged by our new owner?

- **From physicians:** How much disruption is this going to be for me, my office staff, and my patients? Do I have to reapply for privileges? Can I still get my operating room times? Are the clinical protocols the same? Is it simply easier to refer patients somewhere else? What do I tell my patients?
- **From patients:** Can I still see my physician? Will the hospital still have my records? Should I visit another physician until things have settled down? Will my insurance change?
- **From the community:** Will the services remain the same? Will the culture be protected or changed? Will the same nurses or physicians be there for me?

The answers to these questions and the speed with which you can communicate them are vital to building your next strategy.

> The buyer may have similar, coinciding questions, only from an outsider's perspective, including: How quickly can we bring this staff into our culture? How can we help them smoothly transition their standards and procedures to ours? What needs to be preserved at the hospital, and what must change for the partnership to blossom? Will this hospital benefit from bold public branding, or should we move into the community with stealth?

The "New Normal" Campaign

You've spent the past few months promoting the benefits of the combined organizations, introducing the idea of the combined partnership and the good things you'll deliver as a team. In a sense, you've already been selling.

Whether you're the buyer or the seller, now is the time to launch your next campaign. It's time to deliver what you've been pitching.

This is the "new normal" campaign that sets the culture for the combined, new organizations.

Using the Rules in a New Way

Your next task is not merely launching an important relationship-based communications campaign arm-in-arm with your new partner; its success is fundamental to the operational performance of the new partnership.

Fortunately, you already have the tools you need to make that happen. You've been using them all along.

While the rules don't change, how you deploy them may look a little different. Your efforts now are more sustained, even more coordinated, looking even further into the future.

Once you have reached this state, you enter the "lifestyle" of the new organization. Even five years down the road, you will likely still be managing an issue related to the partnership.

The exciting part is that this time is really the start of a new culture for you and your organization.

Here are a few pointers as you enter this new normal.

Start early

Begin planning the communications campaign while you are running the partnership transaction campaign. The day after the documents are signed must be a time of execution, not plan development.

Thankfully, you already have a foundation in place. It may help to assemble a new team or at least assign one person to the new normal campaign so that while you are managing the pre-close communications, that person can focus on the planning for the new work.

Work together with your new partner

This seems obvious, but numerous hospitals ignore the benefit of asking the other hospital to offer insight into their hospital and their community.

You hopefully set the precedent for this in your partnership communications, so the joint communications should really be a natural extension of the work you have already done.

You will likely find that your communications will be richer, more insightful, and more cohesive. In turn, your core audiences will grow their trust in you as a new entity if you acknowledge both where you came from and where you are going as new, forward-looking partners.

Get a baseline

Your plan can be helped by conducting a statistically valid survey of the community to help you determine the expectations created by the partnership. It's your baseline for progress. Think about conducting a survey one month after the papers are signed, so that your core message is likely known but the news is still fresh.

To your audiences, it signals your desire to know their opinion on the partnership. You can use the tool to not only gain their feedback but also to test your core message. Use your core message in the questions you ask so that you can educate while also gaining feedback.

You can revisit the same survey six months or a year down the road to see how perception has changed. Just remember, that old name will stick around for years. It's the feeling about the partnership, the support for the benefits of the merger that you want to test.

Keep your promises

Keeping your promises could take a day, though it will likely take years. This could be the most important piece of your new normal campaign. In your partnership campaign, it's likely you've outlined a number of specific benefits to the joined organizations, such as:

- Capital investments
- New services
- Facility upgrades
- Taxes to be paid
- A foundation to be created

Keep a list of these promises and celebrate when you've achieved each milestone.

This step is as much about messaging as it is about operations. So the relationships you have built among your campaign team, or at least the individuals you tapped for their insights on messages and coordinating your campaign, are still critical. When you can fulfill your promises, everyone celebrates. If there comes a time when promises can't be met, you work on it together, with one united front, to explain why.

Set expectations clearly

In the early days of the new partnership, there will still be many questions that remain unanswerable. Are you going to change the name of the hospital? Will the new partner have a separate advertising budget? Will our organization still sponsor the heart gala next year? Does our organization have specific business development goals?

Be clear about what you know and don't know, and, to the best of your ability, communicate a timetable and a decision process for getting the questions answered. "We should be able to answer that question by early June. Between now and then we'll be working closely with physicians, key staff, and community members to help us determine the best strategies and tactics." It's a classic "We don't have that answer today, but what we do know is ..." response.

Start internally

Getting the talk right inside first is critical here. Everyone will be asking staff and physicians at the newly acquired facility, "What's it like now?"

This means making sure that, with every promise fulfilled, change made, and goal set, your staff and physicians are the first to know. Are there challenges arising under the new partnership? Talk to your staff first before they read about it in the paper. Is there a new benefit to celebrate that you never anticipated (or communicated) would materialize? Celebrate internally first. If it makes sense, a grassroots group can be a good tool to be your eyes, ears, and communicators to your staff in any of these cases.

Reach people at home

The family members of the staff of your new partner facility are a key audience that can support you internally and externally. Target them for special outreach. Welcome them into your new family of hospitals. With their support and buy-in, you also contribute to a happier staff.

For example, host a picnic in the parking lot, invite families to the new signage unveiling, or involve them in a religious service for the hospital if that was or will be part of the tradition of the new entity.

Assume the role on stage

Especially in the early stages of a partnership, you and your leadership team are in the spotlight. Sensitivities are high, hearts are on sleeves, first impressions are made. What you do and don't do, how you carry yourself, what meetings you attend, and how you treat and communicate with others delivers a powerful message. Be strategic in your words and deeds. Deliver the message you intend.

Two Parallel Tracks

Keeping the pointers in the last section in mind, you now have two tracks to run—at the same time.

Internal

Your focus should be on answering (and communicating the answers to) the questions posed at the beginning of this section. Just as in the transaction campaign, your goals include:

- Work collaboratively with your new partner (you both have insights necessary to build a winning campaign)
- Build a core message platform, a theme you can use to rally the troops
- Dissect and prioritize your target internal audiences
- Identify and assign the right messengers to the right audiences
- Surround them with communications
- Pursue them relentlessly

Here are some tactics to meet those goals:

- Extend the life of the deal website to provide frequent updates during the weeks and months following the close. Keep the "ask a question" button live and answer the ones that appear most frequently. Let staff know they can still go to the website to get the most up-to-date information. (Remember: The deal website is public. If the questions/answers are not appropriate for "outsiders," use a more appropriate venue.) You'll know when its time to turn off that site but in the early weeks, it's a helpful resource to you and your audience.

- Consider a quick weekly email from the CEO or a newsletter or poster that gives updates on what's changing and—equally important—what's not. If an email seems old school, consider calling it a blog and posting it on the website or on your intranet. By the same token, if email is still "the wave of the future" for your hospital, physically post the news. Just be sure to keep communicating.
- If your C-suite is new, find ways to meet with employees on their turf. It doesn't have to be formal—in fact, it's best if it isn't. Show up at staff meetings, walk the halls, eat lunch in the cafeteria or in the physician's lounge. Be visible.
- Conduct quarterly town hall meetings. Make sure you cover all shifts. Yes, it's difficult for many associates to attend, but remember, the fact that you're making the effort is a message in and of itself. Record one of the sessions and post the video on your intranet. Then round the hospital to reach out to those who could not attend.
- Research shows that employees trust what they hear from their direct supervisors most of all. Make sure managers and directors are equipped with the

information they need to effectively communicate with their staffs.

External

Your external audiences are watching you carefully, too. Although they clearly have a different perspective than your employees and physicians, it is just as important to let them know how this new partnership is affecting the hospital and the community they know and love.

Your external campaign begins with a candid assessment of your goals for the market, including the answers to these important questions:

- Are you introducing a new brand because of the partnership? For example, "Hospital X is now Hospital Y!"
- Are you strengthening the existing brand to be bigger, better, stronger? "We're still the Hospital X you know and love, now powered by Hospital Y!"

With that decided, then move forward with the tactical ideas:

- An advertising campaign can be the best way to reach the widest audience most quickly. The usual media apply: print ads, billboards, radio spots, television.

Imbed a clear call to action that drives viewers/readers to your website for more information. The themes you have chosen for your internal audiences may or may not be appropriate for an externally facing campaign. Just make sure they don't send conflicting messages.

  - If you are going to include social media as part of your marketing mix, make sure you understand the commitment that such an endeavor requires. Users of social media expect timely two-way communication and don't appreciate being "talked at."

- Don't forget unpaid media. Develop a relationship with the local reporters. Feed the beast with regular updates on your progress.
- Hit the speaking circuit. The local Rotary, Chamber, and Kiwanis will crave the latest information and will be happy to clear a spot on the docket for the CEO, site leader, or other trusted source.
- Support from elected officials and community leaders is important to the ongoing success of your new relationship. Update them with letters and regular face-to-face meetings so they can continue to be your advocates in the community.

- Submit letters to the editor and op-eds from leadership to your local paper, and meet with the paper staff periodically in editorial board meetings. In so many communities, this is a critical step to gaining awareness and support.

Three Phases

With your audiences identified and vehicles thought through, you will need to organize your work. Think of this work in terms of three phases:

- Day one
- First month
- Month two and beyond

Day one

This is the day after your announcement day. Your first step? Round immediately! Then, focus on celebration. Host a party or rally, bring food, celebrate internally together and then invite the community. The hard work will set in quickly, so be sure to enjoy the newness and excitement of the partnership.

First month

Here's where that hard work we referenced starts. Your focus shifts now to the realities of a new partnership and impact on every key stakeholder. While you need to keep a visionary theme to your communications, the focus is on the day-to-day. Your staff asks: "How do we operate in this new environment?" Your patients ask: "Where do I go for treatment?" You will need billboards, a recognition campaign, and the like to make this happen.

If your plan is in place, at least you will only be in execution mode, which will be busy. If you haven't planned, then you have more to do. It's critical that you stick with a communications campaign at this stage and not assume that since you've announced the partnership, the communication is over.

Month two and beyond

There's no end in sight to this phase, because you are now in the mode of celebrating all of the achievements this partnership is making and all of the promises that have been kept. This phase is exciting and tough all at the same time. While you have the chance to celebrate, you also may be facing some course shifts that must be managed as carefully as the entire campaign. Start celebrating small wins—"Everyone has a badge!" "The signs are up!"—and lead up to celebrating significant milestones—"The new, promised cancer center treated its first patient!"

If the Deal Fails

Sometimes a partnership deal falls apart.

The money doesn't work. The cultures don't fit. The politics are wrong. The regulatory environment is ultimately unfavorable to the partnership.

It happens. And if it does, your work continues with the following steps:

1. **Tell it first.** Bad news travels fast. The announcement of a deal going south should be as closely managed as the announcement of a potential partnership. It's not a story that will hold for long, though. Develop your message quickly and move. Cascade your message out to key audiences over the course of a few hours, beginning with your high-priority stakeholders.

   If it does leak, take control quickly. Focus less on finding the leak and more on getting the message fixed and moving forward.

2. **Build a "next step" into your message.** It's not enough to announce that the deal is dead. Have a "so, therefore, we're going to ..." statement that finishes with something tangible, even if that next step is studying further options for the next 90 days.

   It's a signal that your leadership is not fretting, but instead is already looking forward to the next milestone that will accomplish the goals you need to be strong.

   This is not to suggest that you minimize the importance of the partnership that failed; instead, this allows you to also demonstrate that your leadership has a plan—even if it's a stop-gap measure—to protect your hospital.

3. **Explain why the deal failed.** It won't be fun, but the rumor mill will create a story far more dire than the real reasons.

   Remember, you don't have to share or explain confidential details or boardroom politics. That's not what people want, in reality. It is expected, however, that you will share some picture of why the hoped-for marriage didn't occur. Money? Culture? Governance? Regulatory matters?

Additionally, you don't have to attack your former partner to deliver a message that can put the issue to rest so you—and your hospital—can move on.

4. **Walk away together (if you have to walk away).** Joint communications ensure that no one is stabbing anyone in the back on the way out the door. Work together on a common message and, just as important, the timing of its delivery. If you don't, neither party will fare well and be able to take the next steps they need.

5. **Stay true to your vision.** In talking about your potential partnership, it's likely that you've discussed in some detail the threat to your organization if it doesn't embrace change and the bright future that is possible for it through the partnership. To the extent possible, stay true to your vision for your organization. How you will achieve that vision for your organization will certainly change now, but the big picture itself—who you must become to continue your mission—should remain unchanged.

   A note on the threat: It's out there, so your audiences may wonder if you will shut your doors now that this partnership isn't happening. That's why the next-step message is so critical. Likely, your reasons and threats are still the same, but your solution will now look a little different.

6. **Keep moving.** Your competitors may try to take advantage of a failed deal. Don't let them. This can be a vulnerable time for your nurses and physicians. The future they had been planning on will not materialize. What's next for them? Continue to show them your hospital is on the move through your language, your plans, and your personal interactions. Pay close attention to them. This is where your already-established grassroots team can be immensely helpful.

7. **Plan for a drumbeat of continuing communication.** When the partnership was on, you were writing and speaking multiple times a week on the topic. While you may not be at the same frenetic pace if the deal is off, you still need to communicate. One week, one month, a few months down the road, people will want to know what's next. Even if you have not yet identified the right next solution, tell them that. Sharing a message that contains no new news really carries a message that you are in control.

8. **Last, don't be surprised if a celebration erupts.** Change is hard. Merging with a partner is scary and can feel unsafe. While you and your leadership team may have been excited about the potential of a partnership, it may have filled others with dread.

   Acknowledge their relief—change is hard for you, too, after all—but remind them that change must come. The only question to answer is whether you will lead the change, or merely respond when it is forced upon your hospital.

We said it before: Culture is the No. 1 deal killer, so communications—especially in that case—must be done. Even if your partnership is over, your communications campaign is not.

Get Inside Their Head: Unique Considerations for Not-for-Profit Leaders Considering a Partnership

Roughly two-thirds of all hospital mergers and acquisitions (M&A) activity involves two not-for-profit hospitals. There is also a significant number of not-for-profits to investor-owned conversions.

Why do these statistics matter? Because, likely, you will find yourself in the position of needing to understand the unique needs of a not-for-profit organization when you are in the midst of a partnership deal. There are few deals that don't involve one.

These kinds of partnerships require a unique set of considerations. The space is so specialized that some deal advisors make it their sole focus.

Eb LeMaster is one of those advisors. With more than 17 years of experience in investment banking and corporate development, he has completed more than 60 M&A deals. His work focuses on what makes—and breaks—a deal between not-for-profit entities.

LeMaster is the managing director of an eight-member team at Ponder & Co., a nationally recognized advisory firm that works exclusively in the not-for-profit space. The company has completed transactions with some of the most known names in healthcare and some of the largest not-for-profit conversions completed in the past 15 years. Clients range from stand-alone hospitals to large multihospital systems.

While LeMaster's expertise is not communications, his work puts him into contact with communicators who are skilled in that area, and, in his opinion, bring resources to the table that cannot be ignored.

LeMaster answered a few questions about the kinds of issues and considerations that keep his hospital board chairs and CEOs up at night when navigating an M&A deal. His advice, as you will read, elevates and endorses the importance of our work as hospital communicators.

Author: What are some top issues regarding the M&A deal that a not-for-profit leadership team has to think of that an investor-owned leadership team may not?

LeMaster: Not-for-profit boards and management teams are challenged to balance a wide range of issues and constituents when considering alignment strategies. While price is typically the highest priority, the non-financial terms can be as important, or more important, than the price. These include:

- *Mission and service:* Not-for-profits are established with mission and service. This is paramount to all they do. I'll elaborate more on this later, but it's really the first consideration for any M&A deal in this sector of our industry.
- *A wide range of vested constituents:* Not-for-profits must consider the impact of the transaction to a wide range of constituents—patients, physicians, employees, community members, unions, governmental authorities, bond holders, and others. When thinking about these constituents, specifically ask questions such as:
  - How do we carefully define all constituents and try to identify early their vantage point on a potential transaction?

  - Will all employees in good standing be retained for a period of time post-transaction?
  - Will senior staff members be retained or any current contracts assumed?
  - What is the medical staff's position on the potential partner?
  - How do we build and run a thorough and thoughtful process that can withstand scrutiny from a range of constituents?
- *Nonfinancial issues:* In a not-for-profit transaction, nonfinancial factors are as—or more—important. Not-for-profits do not exist to produce the highest return on investment. Instead, even if there is a financial underpinning to the issue, not-for-profits have to think about these questions:
  - How does the board ensure the same level of charity care will continue?
  - What will be the ongoing stake in governance? Will it be meaningful participation at both the local and system level?
  - Will the new owner commit to retaining certain services that are critical to the community?

- Will the buyer recognize the terms of all gifts and property previously made to the hospital?
- What is the proper balance we need to strike throughout the process between financial and nonfinancial outcomes?

- *Long-term results:* In a deal, not-for-profits have a goal not only to maximize up-front and near-term results but also to position the hospital or system for success for many years to come. It is a juggling act. Capital commitment, purchase price, and other financial implications are very important and certainly cannot be ignored, but cultural fit is often of equal importance.

Specifically, in a not-for-profit sale, the transaction can yield a significant foundation that can become important to the local community. These foundations stay around for years. Questions to ask here include:

- What happens to any excess proceeds?
- What capital expenditures will the buyer make post-transaction and when?

- What specific expenditures are included in the commitment? How will the not-for-profit enforce this commitment?

Author: How important are mission, history, and legacy to a not-for-profit community hospital?

LeMaster: These are extremely important. In fact, they are the most important aspect of the deal. Deals fall apart when mission is not first and foremost. Here's why.

Many of these hospitals and systems have been community assets for more than 100 years. The community typically thinks of the hospital as its own asset. You will miss critical communications needs and aspects without a proper understanding of the mission and history.

A key piece of this is gaining a thorough understanding of the founders/sponsors. For example, if the facility has a religious affiliation, it is important to understand what that means, what religious bodies are involved, whether they need to be incorporated in the process, and what approvals will be required. In the Catholic realm, for example, how ethical and religious directive policies and religious indicia are handled post-transaction will depend heavily on the local bishop in a particular community.

Author: What unique pressure does a leadership team face when considering this decision?

LeMaster: Leadership faces the concerns of all the aforementioned constituents—patients to physicians to business leaders, religious affiliations or charity care or foundation proceeds.

Leadership is providing information to the advisors involved, answering questions, facilitating interested parties, handling a range of additional meetings, fielding concerns and questions from physicians and employees, and combatting a bewildering assortment of rumors.

At the same time, leadership of a not-for-profit hospital is also responsible for keeping operations performing at historical levels and keeping the ship from taking on too much water. Running a healthcare organization is challenging enough in the current environment. Searching for a strategic partner at the same time is a huge stress.

All of this happens, in a number of situations, for no additional compensation since C-suite executives have no equity ownership or options to cash out in the case of a sale. Also, although the CEO and executives are very important to decision-making, in many cases, the final decision rests with the board.

Author: What issues typically surprise the buyer when approaching a not-for-profit hospital to purchase?

LeMaster: Timing and pace. Many not-for-profits move slowly and deliberately. The buyer may see obvious benefits to a transaction to both sides, but again, we must remember the leadership and board are handling a community asset that is typically the largest employer in the area. It is a huge decision for those involved and, as a result, the process can be slow.

Buyers can also be surprised by what is most important to a not-for-profit hospital. Financial consideration is always a factor, but a range of subjective factors can be the swing issue. Think about these:

- Is the buyer going to treat our hospital as merely a spoke in the larger wheel of its system?
- What other affiliations do the buyers have?
- Is either party aligned or partnered with a medical teaching institution, and how do our constituents feel about the town-and-gown fit?

It is critical to keep an eye on a wide breadth of topics and issues, because the differences and nuances that drive a decision can stem from a number of areas.

Author: What is one big mental shift that has occurred with the increase in M&A activity in the minds of not-for-profit leaders?

LeMaster: Five years ago, not-for-profit healthcare systems were very reticent to discuss M&A because it implied "selling out" or losing control. With M&A at record levels, that discussion is no longer taboo.

One implication of this new stance, as it relates to your role, is that communications can be more proactive. Many health systems have moved to proactive communications via their website.

Author: Who are typically the kinds of people on a community not-for-profit hospital board? What are their interests?

LeMaster: A community not-for-profit hospital board is typically a strong representation of key organizations, businesses, and interests in that community. The board members are usually leaders in their community—bankers, representatives of religious entities, lawyers, accountants, businessmen and women, retired individuals, physicians, and a range of others.

What's interesting is that they are typically not picked for their healthcare knowledge. They are often picked due to their contribution to or position in the community. Since this is the case, it becomes the job of the board members to collectively balance their perspectives of their respective fields with a not-for-profit, healthcare-focused mission.

Even if a board member has been involved on the board for many years and has learned a great deal about healthcare, he or she is not typically experienced in healthcare M&A. It is difficult in many communities to find such expertise for the board. This is magnified by the fact that the hospitals they represent have not been through a change-of-control transaction in their history.

For example, many community hospitals have bankers who may carry expertise in consolidation. This can be helpful, but healthcare transactions typically have a number of added complexities. Additionally, community boards nearly always include physicians who also try to balance their clinical perspectives with the business side of the hospital's situation.

In contrast, larger systems are able to a greater degree to include board members who may be able to offer specific vantage points. For example, a system may include past top healthcare executives, representatives of major accounting or law firms, leaders in religious healthcare in the nation, and physicians who also have been in leadership positions in the past. Yet, even in this case, the same challenges of balancing objectives exist.

Author: Who are the most critical stakeholders/audiences at play in this kind of a deal? Who has to be won over in order to make it happen successfully?

LeMaster: There isn't one "most" important constituent. The same full range of constituents is important.

Employees are key. The buy-in of community leaders and government officials is essential. And getting started on the right foot is very important as many in the community will develop their opinions of the new owner quickly.

Of particular note in a not-for-profit transaction is that physicians are extremely important. It is a complex issue of how exactly to integrate the physicians in the process due to the various perspectives and the influence the physicians have. But it is critical to have them involved at the right place. The biggest disasters in hospital M&A involve situations when physician support evaporates post-transition or groups leave for other health systems.

Author: What are the most effective communications vehicles when needing to communicate to the hospital's audiences?

LeMaster: Our experience tells us that a good relationship with local press is critical, because that outlet has been covering the hospital for its 100-plus years of service. They are both mainstays in the community. Making sure local press is appropriately in the loop and properly educated is key. The reported story will seldom be 100% accurate, but it is important to get updates to them before they get them elsewhere.

This means that planning communications sooner rather than later is also very important. Many hospitals leave this process for the end. But doing so can lead to firefighting versus proactive planning that anticipates issues and defuses them.

Author: What does a CEO or board chair need to hear from a communications leader in order to elevate communications to a critical piece of the transaction work?

LeMaster: Get organized early. Communications' message to leadership should go along the lines of "We can do it now in an orderly manner, or react later and put out fires."

Being effective in this sell requires designing a process that is thorough and can withstand scrutiny. Many different constituents and people will seek out the CEO and board chair to give them their perspectives. It is a challenge for the CEO and chair to listen to these while also staying focused on the goals. Help them balance the voices that speak out.

Most of all, stay focused on goals that should be established early in the process. There will be many twists and turns. Continue to remind yourself of the original set of goals. That is the scorecard that must guide the process.

Section 4

CASE STUDIES

Reinvented: A New Future for a Community Hospital

Through an acquisition to save a hospital and a transition to an ambulatory care center, Geisinger fought for this critical community resource and the community that needed it.

By David Jolley, vice president, system public affairs, Geisinger Health System

The Challenge

For years, a community hospital hung in limbo. Failing to thrive, Mercy Hospital in Wilkes-Barre, Pa., needed a new solution. Its owner, Catholic Health Partners (CHP), approached different organizations for several years, including Geisinger Health System, but the timing wasn't right. The challenges seemed insurmountable and a solution was never clear.

In 2004, though, CHP approached Geisinger one more time to discuss options; the organizations talked again and took what proved to be the first step in shaping a brighter future for the hospital.

Mercy Hospital's challenges were many, including declining volumes, poor operational performance, lagging information technology, physicians moving patients to another facility, and patients shifting to use more ambulatory and urgent care.

Geisinger, however, saw a way forward for Mercy and completed a deal on December 1, 2005, to make the hospital, now called Geisinger-South Wilkes-Barre (GSWB), part of the Geisinger family. The challenges immediately increased when a major insurer cancelled a key contract that had previously been in place at the hospital.

Geisinger knew from the beginning that moving Mercy Hospital in a new direction would be an uphill battle. In addition to the challenges already named, there was a need to negotiate with an active labor union and a population that wanted to keep its only Catholic hospital in the community. Throughout the partnership discussions and after the close, Geisinger successfully came to a new contract agreement with the unions and also honored the Catholic heritage even though the Catholic identity of the hospital ended.

The acquisition was the right move; yet within a few years after the acquisition it became clear that GSWB needed to provide a new model of care to the community. Patients using the hospital for care in a more transient way proved to be the key to GSWB's future. Making a clear transition to ambulatory and outpatient care—however difficult—would actually meet patient needs better and enable Geisinger to expand its care to more residents.

A key challenge was communicating these two moves.

The Solution

The solution for GSWB began even before a transition was made to a new model of care.

In addition to making an overdue and much needed multi-million-dollar capital investment in the hospital, Geisinger moved forward with a detailed communication plan directed at a number of internal and external target audiences that would be integral to the transaction's success. The communication effort relied on both mass communication and interpersonal face-to-face communication tactics to effectively share messages.

Specifically, Geisinger publicized its investment in the hospital's physical plant, which totaled millions of dollars in repairs, IT infrastructure, and other upgrades. Several local media outlets became key to getting the news out, as well as targeted communications including direct mail and special events.

Geisinger's message, communicated consistently, was that:

- Without very significant changes, the hospital would surely fail.
- Geisinger worked hard to prevent the hospital's closure.
- Geisinger would respect the hospital culture as much as possible. The organization shared this important intention to honor the hospital's long history and the tremendous community service provided by the Sisters of Mercy. Tactically, this took the form of a dedicated Heritage Wall that told the hospital's story and recognized caregivers and the Sisters for their work.

Certainly, Geisinger did what it could in the years after the acquisition. But for a host of clinical and operational reasons, the right model for GSWB could not be found in an acute care setting. The good news was that research showed the community could benefit from a facility solely focused on outpatient and ambulatory care.

Thankfully, Geisinger had built relationships with the community, patients, physicians, the labor union, and religious organizations during the first few years of trying to make GSWB work. These relationships helped during the next round of communications, which began in mid-2008. Similar to the initial acquisition communication, Geisinger shared the news of the transition to the new model of care with targeted audiences and practical messages. Patients, physicians, elected officials, community leaders, business leaders, church leaders, union representatives, and the general public were told—clearly—what would stay at GSWB and what would be accessible at nearby Geisinger facilities.

For employees, Geisinger faced the significant challenge of communicating the loss of approximately 400 jobs. In a community the size of Wilkes-Barre, that amounted to a significant blow. Geisinger worked with employees to place them in other Geisinger Health System locations (approximately 200 people moved into other Geisinger positions), as well as to assist them with outplacement, and communicated this consistently.

The Result

Although the hospital's path to a more promising future was rocky at times, its outlook has improved dramatically, thanks in part to Geisinger's engaged and ongoing communications strategy. Essentially, GSWB is a reinvested and redirected facility and is doing well. The campus is now home to both pediatric and adult urgent care centers, ambulatory surgery, rehabilitation, and other services.

GSWB has reinvented itself, and its outpatient services consistently perform ahead of budget. For example, volume in the urgent care centers is higher than it was when the facility had a full-service emergency department.

Most important, patient feedback is consistently positive and the community recognizes, appreciates, and utilizes GSWB's new model of care.

One State's First For-Profit Conversion, and the People Who Made It Happen

What happens when a not-for-profit community hospital becomes the state's first for-profit conversion?

By Mike Browder, former CEO, Essent Healthcare

The Challenge

In 2000, Sharon (Conn.) Hospital almost closed its doors. The not-for-profit hospital had lost approximately $16 million in the prior six years, and its aging physical plant was in desperate need of repair. Medical staff members were skeptical of the hospital's future, and the local community was losing faith in the organization's ability to deliver quality care. As the only hospital in the region, its fate could have damaged the community.

To save the hospital, the board of trustees proposed selling it to an operator who would bring expertise, capital, and other resources. But this was a dramatic move: It would be the first time an outside, investor-owned company proposed purchasing a hospital in Connecticut. It would be a first test of several state laws regulating the not-for-profit to for-profit conversion.

Overcoming these hurdles was a daunting task, but even more challenging was the prospect of showing the local community how the change would save the hospital and help it prosper.

Almost immediately, some community members voiced their opposition—loudly. In the papers. At community meetings. To the state.

The Solution

The board of trustees knew that the key to a successful future was finding a partner who saw the potential of Sharon Hospital and was willing to invest in the small community. But that partner could not be accepted into the tight-knit community without the support of citizens who could counter the opposition in a credible and sustained way.

The board found both.

In Essent Healthcare of Nashville, Tenn., the board saw the chance to retire the hospital's debt, finance an $8 million renovation, fund a locally controlled community health foundation valued at $20 million, create a sustainable plan for the hospital, establish networks with partnering clinical organizations in the state, enhance obstetrical care for the community, and continue charitable care.

The facts were strong, but the board believed that they were not enough on their own to garner support. The hospital needed advocates. The platform of "fact"—however robust in its investment—needed voices to make it come alive. So the board asked friends, neighbors, leaders—even a few movie stars who happened to call the community home—to step up to the plate.

Over the course of two years, the community rose up in support of the board, its vision, and plan. In fact, two separate community action groups emerged. Hundreds rallied at local hearings to support the hospital. They communicated their position to the leaders in Hartford who would review the deal. Complementing the message of the hospital's dedicated campaign deal team, these groups deployed advertising, direct mail, community forums, rallies, bake-offs, public hearings, civic group presentations, and trips to the state capital.

The Result

As a result of the sale—which may have been derailed without the support of the community—the 78-bed hospital is a financially secure, well-capitalized institution energized by a growing medical staff, an updated physical plant, and an expanding role in the community.

Essent Healthcare made $39 million in capital investments, including facility and equipment, in Sharon Hospital. A new 11,000-square-foot maternity area features advanced technology, two nurseries, and private labor, delivery, recovery, and postpartum rooms. The new emergency department features state-of-the-art technology and private rooms. Physician and staff recruitment and retention have dramatically improved, as have safety, patient satisfaction, and the quality of care. A local governing board, a medical executive committee, and an advisory board also became part of the deal, and it continues its support of the community with services such as free health screenings and direct involvement in more than 25 local groups.

Multiple Hospitals, a Midsize Market, and a Big Transition

Seven hospitals, a new owner, a new ownership structure, a Catholic heritage, a new name ... how each of these critical pieces came together for the benefit of a community's patients and caregivers.

By Jerry Askew, senior vice president, government relations, Tennova Healthcare.

The Challenge

In 2011, Catholic Health Partners (CHP), the owner of the seven-hospital, not-for-profit Mercy Health Partners, embarked on a search to find a new partner for the Knoxville, Tennessee–based system. While the Mercy system had strong roots in Knoxville going back some 80 years, the organization had also gone through significant change, consolidation, and financial struggles for many years.

In a highly competitive healthcare market, the bidding process was heated. But Mercy's board kept its sights on a set of a few core goals in its exploratory process:

- A cultural fit
- A commitment to continue the faith-based organization's Catholic heritage
- A strong capability to manage the multihospital system and help it flourish into the future

Many high-profile not-for-profits and for-profits were vetted in a market where only not-for-profit hospitals existed. Health Management brought significant experience in managing and operating hospitals based in rural and suburban markets. But this would be its largest and most diverse acquisition to date.

A key challenge became convincing the CHP and Mercy boards that Health Management had the skills and smarts to manage a multihospital system in a midsize market. This task also included the ability to work alongside employees, physicians, and the community so that they continued to trust the hospital and its new owner.

The Solution

Health Management needed a plan. It had to demonstrate to the CHP and Mercy boards that it was the right party for Mercy regardless of its perceived limited experience in operating multiple hospital systems. Although this was a larger system in a larger market than Health Management had historically invested in, there were plenty of other qualities that made Health Management a good fit for Mercy.

Health Management's message platform included a set of key points shared through targeted vehicles that:

- Highlighted the company's experience in managing multiple hospitals across multiple states (71 hospitals in 15 states today), rather than focusing on the fact that this one acquisition would be the company's largest.
- Communicated the company's passion, mission, and culture. Leaders were very open and communicated the importance of their faith both personally and as a founding principle of the company.
- Kept a steady drumbeat of communications beyond the initial conversation with the board. Health Management developed a password-protected website

(called "Why Health Management") where board members could learn more about the company, access presentations and plans for Mercy, and watch videos and testimonials of various corporate and hospital leaders. The website was professional, polished, and highlighted a team that was passionate and committed to working with Mercy to meet its vision.

- Introduced CHP and Mercy board members and physicians to Health Management board members and physicians who had gone through similar transitions with Health Management in local hospitals. These members of local hospitals provided a third-party voice endorsing the company's approach and provided testimonials to promises kept.

When it came time to select a partner that fit Mercy's culture and mission—and of course, could provide the necessary capital to move the organization forward—Health Management was clearly the best fit.

Once the decision was made for Health Management to acquire Mercy, the work began to allay any fears of change among leadership, associates (Health Management's preferred word for "employees"), and physicians, and to sincerely convey all the reasons that Health Management was the right partner for the hospitals.

To start, Health Management and Mercy worked together to communicate within and outside the organization. From this point on, the organizations were working from the same plan and set of messages. Health Management was on-site and working hand-in-hand with leadership, associates, and physicians from day one, involving them in each step of the due diligence process leading up to the expected October 2011 closing. Individual, in-person interaction was particularly important so that Health Management was not portrayed as a distant team controlling the Knoxville–based system from an office in Naples, Fla. A large team from Health Management was in the market and stayed there throughout the transition; this helped to humanize Health Management and to form a relationship early on.

Health Management also explained the company's history as one based on Christian principles, described the mission, vision, and guiding principles—and instilled a sense of hope in Mercy's team that their Catholic history and traditions would live on under Health Management's leadership. In fact, the Sisters of Mercy, who had long been with the organization, were encouraged to stay to help minister in the system for as long as they would like.

As part of the agreement with CHP, the Mercy name would change on the day of closing. Health Management engaged with leadership, associates, physicians, and members of the community to ensure they felt a sense of ownership in creation of the system's new name.

More specifically, Health Management needed to cover a lot of ground (literally and figuratively) in the three months between signing the letter of intent and closing the deal. It had seven hospitals with 5,000 associates and 1,100 physicians scattered across five counties, so communicating evenly and simultaneously across the system would be a difficult task.

First, Health Management launched a separate website (www.MercyIn2Great.com), which was solely dedicated to communicating the details of the partnership and what it meant for Mercy's associates, physicians, and the community. This ensured communication of a consistent message to a large, geographically dispersed audience who could access the site from work or home. It became the single best source of information on the transaction, for questions to be asked and answered, and for updates to be provided in a timely way.

Second, at each key milestone in the process, including the letter of intent, definitive agreement, name change, and deal closing, Health Management hosted simultaneous events at each of the system's locations with key Health Management leadership present. This made each hospital, regardless of its location, feel equally important and ensured that each hospital received the same information at the same time.

Other methods of communication included associate and physician-specific meetings and events, rounding on the floors, face-to-face meetings, regular updates through email and newsletters, and the creation of strong news media relationships.

The Results

When the deal closed on time in October 2011, Health Management was a friend to Mercy. There was a trust and belief that Health Management was there to move the organization forward.

When the name officially changed to Tennova Healthcare on closing day, associates felt invested in this next chapter of their organization's life. Tennova was specifically chosen to represent the geographic location, as well as derived from the

Latin word "novare," which means to make new. Both meanings carried significance to the health system.

On the one-year anniversary, Health Management had exceeded its commitments to the community with a total economic impact of $413 million, more than $15 million in state and local property and sales taxes, and an increase in patient visits to its hospitals, including a 3.4% increase in emergency department visits and an 11% increase in inpatient surgeries.

Health Management may be based in Florida, but it plays an active role in the East Tennessee community now—as it does in all its hospital markets. Early results show that starting off the right way in the community by building relationships makes all the difference in strong growth and performance.

Glossary

asset purchase agreement: The asset purchase agreement is the written document explaining the sale of one hospital to another. It is a lengthy contract that serves as the legal means for executing a merger or acquisition. It sets the terms of the deal.

certificate of need (CON): A CON is the approval given by a local or state agency for the proposed construction or expansion of a hospital. Not all states have a CON process, which means that in some states anyone can add healthcare facilities to a community. Where it is required, there is a state-specific process that a hospital or healthcare entity must follow in order to start its project. It usually involves a series of plans, needs study, community support, and other official filings. The purpose of the CON is to prove that the hospital is necessary and to ensure that medical services are not duplicated. A CON process can take a few months, but in cases where a competitor in the area appeals it, it can take up to several years.

change of sponsorship: A change of sponsorship occurs when the original founders of a hospital sell the organization.

Often you hear the term when discussing the conversion of a Catholic hospital system to a non-Catholic system. At issue in these scenarios are topics like whether the new owner will honor ethical and religious directives of the Catholic hospital or keep representation of the original owners on the board.

community foundation: A community foundation can be formed from the proceeds of a deal where a not-for-profit is purchased, mainly by a for-profit organization. It is often set up on an endowment model, where the interest earned is used to address the healthcare needs of a community. Foundations can be governed by members of the hospital board in a separate entity.

deal team: A deal team usually consists of each hospital's internal leadership working together with outside accountants, attorneys, investment bankers, and brokers to complete a hospital transaction. It is similar to a campaign team mentioned in this book, but usually precedes any involvement by communications.

Federal Trade Commission (FTC) review: After hospitals report a proposed deal, the FTC conducts a preliminary review to decide if the agreement should be approved. The FTC's primary goal is to watch for the potential of monopolistic activity, keeping the community in mind. During this review, the hospitals must wait 30 days before the deal can close. Based on what the FTC finds, it can: 1) end the waiting period and allow the hospitals to complete the deal (aka early termination); 2) let the waiting period run out, then allow the hospitals to complete the deal; or 3) if the FTC finds issues in the review, it may extend the review period and require that more information be provided about the transaction (aka second request).

integration teams: Once a deal is closed, an integration team is usually created to ensure a smooth transition between the organizations. These are functional teams that are clinically and organizationally trained to work with staff, materials management, facilities operators, and others to make sure that systems are working and processes are set that make sense for the future.

memorandum of understanding (MOU): The MOU is often the first stage in the formation of a contract. It outlines the terms of an agreement between hospitals and sets in motion a formal exploratory process. It can be a binding or nonbinding document. It becomes binding when it includes the "four corners": offer, consideration, intention, and acceptance, typically when due diligence is completed.

regulatory approval: The regulatory environment consists of many multilayered agencies. The approval of a deal must go through the necessary local, state, or federal approval processes before the deal can move forward. For healthcare professionals, this means that considerable attention to detail in the planning and implementing of a deal is vital.

task force: A task force is a temporary group of people formed to carry out a specific project, or to solve a health-care provider's problem in a timely manner. Task forces are created to help healthcare systems solve crises on an as-needed basis.